Helping Your Children Love Each Other

Helping Your Children Love Each Other

Joyce Milburn

BETHANY HOUSE PUBLISHERS
MINNEAPOLIS, MINNESOTA 55438
A Division of Bethany Fellowship, Inc.

The Scripture quotations, unless otherwise noted, are taken from the New International Version of the Bible.

Published by Bethany House Publishers
A Division of Bethany Fellowship, Inc.
6820 Auto Club Road, Minneapolis, MN 55438

Printed in the United States of America

Library of Congress Cataloging in Publication Data

Milburn, Joyce, 1953-
    Helping your children love each other.

    Includes bibliographical references.
    1. Children—Conduct of life. 2. Parent and child. I. Title.
BJ1631.M64   1983   248.8'4   83-15505
ISBN 0-87123-307-X (pbk.)

The Author

JOYCE MILBURN received her B.A. in Christian Education in 1976. She then became a natural childbirth instructor and founded Genesia Childbirth Educators. She is co-author of *The Natural Childbirth Book* (Bethany House, 1981) and currently resides in Southern California with her husband and three sons.

Table of Contents

Foreword

Creating the right atmosphere in the home—how important it is! I'm glad Joyce Milburn is writing on this vital subject.

John 12:3 tells us that when Mary poured perfume on the feet of Jesus, "the house was filled with fragrance." There should be such an atmosphere in every home where Jesus is loved! Guests will sniff the air—and will notice.

And the children will notice, too. School may be threatening, relationships with peers competitive, but home can be the place they run to for support and security. When they tumble in that front door, the air can "smell good."

As you expose yourself to Joyce Milburn's insights on the subject, you're doing yourself a favor!

Anne Ortlund
Corona del Mar, California

Introduction

After having read *The Natural Childbirth Book** (which I co-authored with Lynnette Smith), a friend said to me, "I enjoyed it, but what I'm waiting for is the sequel: *What To Do with 'em Now That You've Got 'em!*" She, as most of us, had discovered the work of parenting doesn't end in the delivery room; it only begins there.

On our first wedding anniversary, my husband and I celebrated in grand fashion, for we had often heard, "If you make it through the first year you can make it through *anything*." We congratulated ourselves on succeeding at marriage and proceeded blithely on, no longer "working at it." We discovered very quickly that one cannot be passive about a person he loves. If the relationship is not making steady, upward progress (even though slow), it is headed the other direction—downhill and fast.

This applies also to the children in our families. As the boys and girls quarrel and squawk in the next room, we parents often roll our eyes, plug our ears, and yawn, saying, "Ho-hum, they're at it again. Oh well, I guess there's nothing we can do about it; it's a natural part of growing up."

That is only a half-truth. Competition between siblings is certainly natural. But childhood is a person's initiation into the human race and it is a time of learning many things. One of the things he must learn, in order to survive and succeed in the adult world, is how to live, work, and play side-by-side with those who are different from himself.

Children are real people; younger and smaller than we adults are, but real just the same. And the childhood years are a perfect time for helping them learn how to build relationships with other

---

*Bethany House Publishers, 1980.

real people, beginning with their brothers and sisters.

Christian family authorities with a wide spectrum of views on other subjects seem to intersect in full agreement on this point: While sibling rivalry can never be erased, it *can* be controlled. God's Word instructs us to "live at peace with everyone" (Rom. 12:18). We therefore must *train* our children to love each other. But such love doesn't come naturally any more than a happy marriage or robust physical fitness—all good things are the result of hard work. But the satisfaction is always worth the effort.

In preparing this book, I have interviewed dozens of parents, teachers, and child specialists (I would not be so presumptuous as to tell you how to raise your children from my experience alone). But I do feel comfortable integrating my ideas with the thoughts of those who may be further along in the battle. I hope you'll join them and me as we explore "what to do with 'em now that we've got 'em!"

1

Is This the Impossible Dream?

As I rubbed the sleep from my eyes, long fingers of sunlight reached past dancing brown leaves and into our bedroom. Such a clear November morning would usually invigorate me. But after a rather uncomfortable night, I felt just as I had every morning for the past several months—*very* pregnant. It was the last Sunday in November; I was now past my ninth month.

As I rolled (literally) out of bed, my mind filled with thoughts of all the things to be done before church. Christopher, almost three, needed a bath and breakfast. I had to set my hair and decide which of the two dresses that still fit me I would wear that day. I needed to gather my thoughts and my teaching materials so I could pass them on to my replacement in the three-year-old Sunday school class. I also had to fold and put away Saturday's laundry, and the floor could stand to be vacuumed. To top things off, Ralph, my husband, had been up most of the night with some dastardly flu. He would be of little help.

Despite the list of activities that awaited my attention, I felt a new surge of enthusiasm for the tasks, a lightheartedness, a radiance. My due date had come and gone and I knew that soon my longing arms would cradle someone very special: our second child.

My thoughts drifted to the coming event. *Christmas will be here soon—what a special time of year to be having a baby. I wonder how soon it'll be.* . . . Little did I suspect "it" would occur so soon. Less than two hours later, labor had commenced and Ralph was making the fastest recovery from flu on record.

By 9:00 that night, my musings of just a dozen hours before had become a reality. A warm and huggable Jonathan dozed contentedly at my breast and we were a happy family of four.

Christopher, who has always been an enthusiastic and exhuberant child, reacted very positively to his new brother. Glowing with pride, he tenderly stroked Jonathan's soft, velvety skin. He held him and talked to him in high-pitched whispers. He kissed him, hugged him, and brought him "s'prizes."

Pleased with our older son's warm reaction, it was easy for Ralph and me to bask in the glow of God's love and goodness. Although newspaper headlines would not have borne this out, at least in my eyes all was well with the world. It certainly was well with our family. That night a new dream entered my mind, and we whispered a prayer, "Lord, make this love *last*."

Actually, that dream goes back quite some time. At the risk of exposing myself to ridicule, I would like to reveal some early illusions I had before I became a mother of even one child. (My husband has always been a more realistic person, and insists that I be honest in emphasizing that these were *my* dreams, not *ours*.)

I figured we would have from two to four children, probably all boys, but not like any boys I had ever known. For in my mind's eye, at least, these fellows were docile and cooperative, yet strong-willed, gregarious, and creative leaders. They would always be absorbed in projects that did not require my direct supervision, yet I would find them willing to drop everything and come running at my first beckoning. They would, of course, play outside all day (someone told me boys do that) and this would free me for a variety of creative endeavors—such as sewing clothes and baking bread. At dinner time they would come in with shining faces and combed hair. They would avoid dirt and grease in the same way their mommy does, but I knew that when they grew up they would be athletic and mechanically-minded like their dad. Our sons would have no desire to use such loathsome objects as toy machine guns, but as adults I was sure they would be proud to help defend their country. These boys would be angels in blue jeans. And best of all, they would be so devoted to one another that cross words would never leave their lips or even enter their minds.

There is, of course, no need for you to harbor any illusions about our family being perfect. Only two parts of the vision even approximate the truth: we have three children and they are all boys (number three having arrived after this book was written).

We enjoy watching our sons' relationships develop and grow as their bodies do. Like brothers everywhere, they have their moments, both good and bad. And like most parents, we're happiest when there are more good moments than bad ones.

I've found that most parents share similar feelings. They all want their children to love each other, but many parents are uncertain of what can be done to make it happen. However, as an avid reader, I discovered that many respected Christian professionals have addressed the subject of sibling rivalry. But sifting through stacks of child-rearing books and tapes takes *time*—a precious commodity these days for any parent.

One psychologist has suggested facetiously that someone should hold a convention for all the traumatized parents of two-year-olds so that they could compare notes. A similar convention, for parents of kids who fight, would probably prove most enlightening, but most parents could not attend because they are too busy being full-time referees!

Perhaps this book will serve as a "convention." Together we will explore authorities' and parents' views on what factors help children live together in harmony. I sincerely believe that the solutions which have worked for others will also work for you.

"Come on," you may be saying about now. "Can we really teach my child (who thinks his mission in life is to make himself an *only* child) how to be loving and respectful to his sisters and brothers?"

To that I answer, "Can you teach him to eat with a fork and spoon, to make a bed, to do his homework on time?" Maybe not with ease, and perhaps not to the desired level of perfection, but *yes, he can learn*. For as Dr. Niles Newton has remarked, "Pleasantness is largely a set of good habits."[1] A habit is *learned*.

Dr. James Dobson writes, "One of the primary responsibilities of parents and teachers (especially those within the Christian faith) is to teach children to love one another. It *can* be done."[2]

All right. If it can be done, *how* is it done? As I asked parents what they were doing about sibling rivalry, an interesting pattern emerged: the parents who gave the darkest tales of woe had more or less resigned themselves to their children's bickering and weren't doing much to curb, control, or shape attitudes. On the positive side, many parents said, "Sibling rivalry isn't a big problem at our house"—and they were able to tell me *why*. They were applying certain principles to insure that their children got along well. They were using an active, rather than passive, approach. They had dedicated themselves to licking the problem, or preventing it, and they were succeeding.

My research began with question marks, but ended with exclamation points. Yes! Sibling rivalry can be controlled, and average parents, just like you and I, are finding the solutions to the problem.

2

God Is a Perfect Parent

The young mother threw down her dish towel in exasperation and stormed into the living room. As soon as she entered, her five-year-old daughter scurried to the couch, mischief lighting her face. Her little brother stopped his tormented screams and they eyed each other with sidelong glances, each looking guilty yet somehow triumphant. Although they usually played quite well together, the two had been squabbling for the better part of the day, and both seemed to sense that this time they had pushed Mom too far.

The woman fumed at her older child. "Why do you keep teasing him like that? You never used to treat Daniel that way."

The girl twisted up her face in consternation and pondered the question for a brief moment. Then, blue eyes solemn, she replied, "The reason I never used to treat him like that is because *we never used to have him*."

Sometimes it may seem that the simplest solution to sibling rivalry is to not have more than one child—or to keep apart forever the ones you do have. One mother, knowing of my interest, wrote, "After observing our two, kind, sweet, loving daughters, we've come to the conclusion that they get along best in small groups—preferably of no more than one." She wrote it in jest, but there is a thread of truth in that statement that most of us can identify with. Part of God's design for the universe was for people to dwell in families. Yet, with every member added to a family, the number of relationships to be nurtured multiplies. A family of three has only three relationships to cultivate: husband-wife, mother-child, and father-child. A family of five, on the other hand, has more—ten to be exact. A household of ten members juggles a potpourri of forty-five different relationships, each requiring the constant give-and-take of family life. This can get complicated!

The Bible indicates that sibling rivalry is one of the oldest problems of mankind, having been chronicled since the very first pair of brothers brought happiness and havoc to the home of Adam and Eve. Scripture is replete with accounts of brothers and sisters who evidently had trouble adjusting to one another. Some of those notorious relationships were incredible enough to rival Hollywood's slickest offerings. The emotions involved range from what seems to be a mild personality clash between Mary and Martha (while Jesus was their guest) to bitter hostility that caused Absalom to murder Amnon. We need to consider a few of these instances.

Cain and Abel, the first siblings ever, were boys with widely differing interests and abilities. Little is written in Genesis 4 about their relationship, but scholars believe Cain's hatred for his younger brother stemmed from the fact that Cain was willfully disobeying a commandment previously given by God. When Abel obeyed, this aroused Cain's ire, for he probably felt that it made him "look bad." John gives us insight regarding these feelings when he poses the question and gives an answer: "And why did he murder him? Because his own actions were evil and his brother's were righteous" (1 John 3:12). He chose to eliminate the competition in cold blood. After this first sibling relationship ended in such a grisly manner, one might hope to see things improve from there on. Unfortunately, several other families seemed to have problems just as great.

Not too many generations later, we learn of Abraham's sons, the half brothers Ishmael and Isaac. Again, the details of the boys' relationship are rather sketchy, but Genesis 21 tells us that at one point Sarah became very upset after having witnessed Ishmael mocking, or making fun of, her son Isaac. She insisted that Ishmael and his mother move out. Unfortunately, this family feud has lasted longer than that of the the Hatfields and McCoys. Isaac, through Jacob, became a forefather of the nation of Israel; Ishmael became the progenitor of the Arab people. The front page of today's newspaper is all the evidence needed to prove that the hostility has never ceased.

After Ishmael left, Isaac probably had a few years of peace and quiet, but once he married Rebekah and had children of his own, his life was again tainted by strife. Esau and Jacob, the couple's twin sons, were as different as two kids could be, and intensely competitive (not unlike the parents). We are told in Genesis 25 that their parents each had a favorite son, which undoubtedly fanned the fires of competition. Esau, the rugged outdoorsman and hunter, was most loved by his father, while Jacob, a quiet, indoor person, was a "Mama's boy." There must also have been problems between Isaac and Rebekah, because she was quick to conspire with her favored son to deceive her own husband!

Jacob, with his mother's encouragement, deceived his father in order to gain the patriarchal blessing reserved for Esau. When Esau learned that he had been cheated out of his inheritance, he was understandably angry and bitter. So bitter was he, in fact, that he resolved to kill Jacob. Jacob's only recourse was self-imposed exile.

Ironically, Jacob's adult life was besieged by sibling difficulties on two other levels: his wives and his sons. Jacob fled the country and took up residence with Laban, a maternal uncle. He then met his beautiful cousin, Rachel, and arranged to work for her father seven years in exchange for her hand. The wedding took place as planned, but when Jacob awoke the next morning he discovered *he* was the victim of trickery. His father-in-law had replaced Rachel with Leah because it was considered a disgrace for the younger sister to marry before the older one. Upset but undaunted, Jacob worked an additional seven years and acquired Rachel.

The relationship between the two sisters was never pleasant. Leah conceived child after child for Jacob, but Rachel was barren for many years. Eventually she did conceive and bore a son.

One might think Jacob would have learned from his own

unhappy childhood how damaging it can be to have a "favorite" child, but apparently he did not. Genesis 37 tells us that Jacob's favorite (of his twelve sons) was Rachel's firstborn, Joseph.

Jacob "loved Joseph more than any of his other sons, because he had been born to him in his old age; and he made a richly ornamented robe for him. When his brothers saw that their father loved him more than any of them, they hated him and could not speak a kind word to him" (Gen. 37:3, 4). The boys' resentment of Joseph drove them to plot his murder. Mercifully, the eldest brother, Reuben, convinced them that throwing him into a prison-like pit would be just as effective; another brother persuaded them that if they sold him as a slave, they would not only make a tidy profit but be free of the guilt of murder. The end of this story is happier than most, but that we will discuss later in this book.

If we were to stop reading here, we would have a highly inaccurate view of the biblical model for siblings. We might readily conclude that brothers and sisters are for hating, and that we parents can do nothing about it. This is not true. Of course, the Bible also portrays some beautiful, touching accounts of brothers and sisters who loved each other, and therefore cared for one another, worked together and held the sibling bond as something dear.

Consider Miriam, who watched near the banks of the Nile to see what would happen to her baby brother Moses. When Pharaoh's daughter discovered that the drifting basket of reeds contained a helpless Hebrew infant and decided to raise the child as her own, Miriam suddenly appeared and offered to locate a wet-nurse for the babe. She, of course, "found" the boy's own mother. Miriam was just a young girl, yet she participated in a very risky scheme to save her brother from genocide with no concern for herself.

Later we see the close bond between Moses and his brother Aaron when the Lord used them to lead the children of Israel out of Egypt. Moses, feeling inadequate for the task, claimed he wasn't eloquent enough to lead a nation. God therefore teamed him up with Aaron, using Aaron as the spokesman for the messages God gave to Moses. Still later we see how God used all three siblings, Moses,

Aaron, and Miriam, to coordinate the exodus from Egypt. Only one instance of conflict between them is recorded (Num. 12).

The New Testament tells of brothers who managed to get along well enough to form business partnerships. James and John fished together day in and day out as adults. So did Simon Peter and Andrew. Andrew cared so much about Peter that when he came to the realization that Jesus Christ was the Messiah, his immediate concern was that his brother meet Jesus. "The first thing Andrew did was to find his brother Simon and tell him, 'We have found the Messiah. . . .' Then he brought Simon to Jesus. . ." (John 1:41, 42).

An often overlooked message of the unity that is possible between siblings lies in the scriptural use of the word "brother." It depicts an intimate, loving bond. In the Old Testament, "brother" almost always referred to a blood relative. The most well-known exception to this is the close comradeship between David and Jonathan. When Jonathan was killed, David lamented, "I grieve for you, Jonathan my *brother*; you were very dear to me" (2 Sam. 1:26).

In New Testament times, "brother" or "sister" was frequently used as a term of endearment, not in reference to flesh and blood relationship. This implication can be interpreted in either of two ways: first, that brotherhood and sisterhood are the closest, most intimate ties imaginable; second, that in Christ, as children of God, we are *all* brothers and sisters.

God is the perfect parent. He is loving, protective, and sensitive to our every need, yet firm, honest, and fair. Our Heavenly Father's care for us embodies the prime example of everything an earthly parent could ever hope to be. According to the Bible we, His children, are "brothers" and "sisters" of His other children.

God has given us page after page of tender parental guidance on how we are supposed to love our spiritual siblings. Could He possibly mean for us to love flesh and blood siblings to any lesser degree? Of course not. While many young brothers and sisters would deny the fact, their siblings are fellow human beings, and are worthy of being treated as such. I would dare say that there is not one biblical admonition about loving others that should not first be applied in the home.

Consider the book of Romans, a feast of detailed instruction for Christian life and service. Chapter 12 alone offers these morsels of wisdom:

> In Christ we who are many form one body, and each member belongs to all the others. Love must be sincere. Hate what is evil; cling to what is good. Be devoted to one another in brotherly love. Honor one another above yourselves. Share with God's people who are in need. Practice hospitality. Rejoice with those who rejoice; mourn with those who mourn. Live in harmony with one another. Do not be proud, but be willing to associate with people of low position. Do not be conceited. Do not repay anyone evil for evil. Be careful to do what is right in the eyes of everybody. If it is possible, as far as it depends on you, live at peace with everyone (vss. 5, 9, 10, 13, 15-18).

The words of Scripture seem to assume that love can be fostered between virtually *any* two people if desire and willingness are present.

One of our goals as parents should be to see this close-knit bond of "brotherly" affection produced between our own children as an outgrowth of the spiritual training we provide them. Such love is not a pipe dream.

It can exist in our homes. In the next chapter we'll take a long, objective look at the problems some families experience and try to discover what causes them.

Throughout this book you will find discussion-starters, designed to help you think about what you have read and help you apply it to your family. *Parent Talk* questions are designed for you to think through alone, or discuss with your spouse. *Family Time* activities are for the entire family to work on together. For *Family Time*, set aside an unhurried period when all family members are together. It is important to keep all discussions positive in nature, avoiding critical and demeaning remarks. No child should be permitted to say anything negative about another child at these sessions.

Parent Talk

1. We have spoken of God as being the perfect parent. On paper, list as many "parental" qualities of God as you can think of.

2. Which of the qualities you have listed would your children probably like to see more of in you?
3. Pray together about each of these qualities, asking the Lord to make you the parents He wants you to be.

Family Time

1. Discuss: How does God want us to treat others? How do we know this? (Have the children quote verses or give examples if they can.)
2. Let each child recall a time when he or she was treated kindly by another family member.
3. Read Eph. 4:32 together. Discuss: Does "one another" include brothers, sisters and parents?
4. What are some ways by which we could show more love within our family?

3

Cause and Effect

I have a brown thumb. Therefore our neighbors rarely ask me to plant-sit while they go on vacation. And my husband knows better than to bring me a houseplant—unless he has a death wish for it. Vegetation may thrive merrily on anyone else's windowsill, but let *me* care for it, and it soon will be a droopy stalk.

Not long ago, I nearly caused the demise of an innocent aphelandra. (This plant, incidentally, held a record in our home; it had lived with us nearly two years. The reason for its longevity, I believe, is that I avoided looking at it, much less touching it. Ralph watered it daily, and it seemed to delight in the sunshine through our kitchen window.)

One morning, I discovered a thick trail of ants parading through that window and straight into the aphelandra's pot. *Horrors!* I thought. *The little wretches are building a nest in my house.* An idea flashed through my mind: Flood the beasts out. After all, a little water never hurts a plant—does it? With great glee I watched hundreds of ants struggle over the pot's edge and down the kitchen drain. I was not nearly so jubilant the next morning, however, when I found the normally straight-as-an-arrow plant drooping sadly to one side, all the leaves dark and floppy. My zealous watering had been as lethal to the plant as to the ants. Although I've never seen the roots of our aphelandra, the leaves and stem offered clear evidence that something was wrong below the surface. I'm happy to report that after tending that sickly plant for about six weeks, it made a full recovery!

I had brought on the aphelandra's problems through my lack of concern for the roots. I had not even touched the leaves or stem, yet they manifested the ill effects of my thoughtlessness toward the roots.

So it is with our children. The "fruit" we see in their lives (their behavior) is evidence of what is taking place internally. We therefore have two choices. Either we can be one step ahead of the game, caring for their "root needs," or we can always be several steps behind, trying to improvise a cure after it's too late to do much good. Bickering and fighting are usually just the fruit of problems festering deep within. Dr. Bruce Narramore explains:

> Day after day, and week after week we are spending countless hours telling, correcting, or instructing our children *after* they have gotten into trouble. Gradually and almost imperceptibly, parenting becomes a hassle. Because we are so busy correcting our children, we find ourselves spending less time together just having fun together or enjoying each other's company.
>
> I call this the "fire engine approach" to parenting. We try to put out one fire after another, but always *after* trouble has begun.[3]

A conscientious fire marshall can detect faulty wiring or combustible material *before* they become four-alarm emergencies. His knowledge and expertise help building owners eliminate possible causes and thus create an atmosphere of safety. It is almost always easier to attempt prevention beforehand than to fumble for a solution after things have gotten out of control.

This principle may be further illustrated by the treatment allergists provide for their patients. My husband and I have severe allergies, so we make regular trips to a local doctor, who gives us injections to prevent attacks of asthma and hay fever. Some people do not understand why having shots every couple of weeks is preferable to just taking a pill after problems develop. However, after many years of struggling with these ailments, we have found we are far more comfortable and happy with a preventive approach.

Because of their parents' physical problems, our sons are highly susceptible to allergic diseases. Our doctor, therefore, outlined specific steps we should take with our sons to minimize their chances of incurring breathing troubles. These measures deal mainly with the quality of the air—the physical atmosphere—in our home. We keep our grass mowed short and our windows closed. We have no pets (except a few fish, who seem to pose no threat). We use no wool or other fibers that might cause difficulty. The boys' room is practically bare, so that dust won't build up.

Food is also a factor. I breastfed each for a long time in the interest of avoiding allergies. I'm now glad I did. Both showed reactions to cow's milk when it was introduced.

Physicians tell us that while a person may remain allergic all his life, adequate treatment in advance can ward off many severe attacks. Similarly, James Dobson once remarked that, like allergies, "sibling rivalry is difficult to cure, but it can certainly be treated."[4]

Our treatment will be directed at the underlying *causes* of trouble, in cleaning up the "atmosphere" at home. This will not be the physical climate, of course, but the *emotional* and *spiritual* surroundings. Why be satisfied with plucking defective fruit off the family tree, only to ignore the rotting roots? Why keep sending the fire engines if the blazes can be prevented? Why content ourselves with allergy pills if we can forestall their necessity?

Let's return to our Bible siblings again to explore some of the causes we'll be treating. Although centuries have passed since these people lived, people remain essentially the same, and hindsight's vision is usually 20/20. The Bible points out many reasons for their behavior, most of the reasons being the same for today's sibling problems.

Attention

Some children feel, as Joseph's brothers must have felt, threatened by the presence of a younger child. The older sibling may have been so young when the competitor arrived that he could not understand why his parents could love more than one child. Or, like

Ishmael, he may have been old enough to rationalize that a new addition would divide his parents' time and assets. This turmoil of feelings will be amplified when one parent or both spend a large amount of time with the infant—time which used to belong to the older child.

The drive to gain a parent's attention is probably the most obvious reason for sibling mistreatment. Especially in these days when time is at such a premium, parents who have their schedule full of outside interests may find it difficult to give each child the attention he or she craves, and deserves.

Inequality

Maybe our children are more like Rachel and Leah—unequally matched in terms of beauty, talent, brains, charm, physical abilities, or other attributes. If the spotlight continually shines on one child while the other always seems to warm the bench, a spirit of competition may develop. My sister and I, as teenagers, faced such a situation. We spent quite a bit of time with a nice boy from our youth group. We had many good times together until one day, meaning to compliment us, he blurted out that my sister was "sure good looking" but that I had "all the personality." As well-intentioned as his remarks were, it was a no-win statement. We both felt like clobbering him, and afterward our friendship was never quite the same.

Some parents unwittingly fuel this conflict in much the same way. Have you ever heard a parent introduce his children in this way: "This is Fred, our athlete, and here's Frank, the smart one." While both descriptions certainly sound complimentary, they subtly point out each child's deficiencies as well. Other remarks can be equally damaging: "Why can't you stay out of trouble like your sister Mary?" or "Your brother never flunked anything in high school."

Self-esteem

Often a low self-image will cause a child to misbehave. Children who feel inferior to others often resort to trickery or force to achieve a sense of superiority. Self-esteem may have been a part of Jacob's problem. He knew his father loved Esau more and that Esau was destined to receive the family blessing. Jacob may have felt so inferior that he convinced himself there was nothing legitimate he could do to win his father's favor—so he resorted to devious tactics.

A low opinion of oneself can result from any number of circumstances. A genuine lack of ability (usually physical or mental) is only one. Many children ar highly competent, even superior, physically and mentally, but have low self-images because of cruel words and unkind remarks made by adults or other children. Remember, Isaac and Rebekah didn't hide their favoritism at all! We must be more careful than they to not let our children feel insignificant or useless. We will discuss this subject in depth later on.

Parental Example

Another contributing factor in Jacob's problem was the example set by his parents. Isaac and Rebekah had a troubled marriage. Rebekah's open hostility toward her husband indicates that they were not on the best of terms.

Children learn how to cope with people and incidents largely by watching how we, their parents, react in the same situations. Some children quibble and quarrel because that is what they see their parents doing most of the time; it therefore seems the most natural, convenient way to solve disagreement.

Teaching

As evidenced in the life of David and his children, there is sometimes a great lack of home teaching in regard to godly character. Look closely at David's life as king. Scripture tells us that he had at least eight wives and many unnamed concubines. Scholars believe that he fathered at least 21, and possibly as many as 50 children. Spending time with each child would have been nearly impossible. In addition, his duties as king of Israel had him carrying the burdens of an entire nation upon his shoulders. (And we think *we* have it rough, trying to manage a household, a marriage, a couple of kids, and a job or two!) David doubtless had little spare time to train his many children, and he had even less time to work on the atmospheres in his various homes. The results were tragic. Although David was a chosen servant of God, his children's escapades would make today's soap operas look tepid (e.g. 2 Sam. 13).

Most of today's parents are extremely busy; one day merges into the next at breakneck speed. It's easy to fall into a rut of saying, "Just as soon as this project is over, I'll settle down and take time with the kids," or "If we can ever get caught up on all our bills we won't have to work such long hours." It becomes easy to hand over a child's spiritual training to Sunday school teachers or a Christian school. But these institutions do not relieve a parent from the God-given responsibility to "train up a child."

Diverse Opinions

Many children (and adults too) argue just because they don't see eye to eye. A good example of this might be Mary and Martha, sisters whose differing priorities led to a tiff recorded in Luke 10. Jesus was a guest in their home, and while Martha bustled about, cooking and serving, Mary made herself comfortable and engaged their visitor in conversation. This irritated Martha, so she vented her opinion.

I consider this the least harmful type of sibling conflict. In fact, it can't even be classified as "rivalry" because differing opinions can often rise between two people who may love each other very much. Someone has said, "If two people agree on everything, one of them is not necessary." While it can be most annoying to see two children repeatedly disagree, parents can use such an incident as an occasion for teaching that there is a right way to argue—with respect and consideration for the other person and his viewpoint.

Other reasons children have for fighting are not so clearly exemplified in the Bible, but are still valid.

Boredom

Some children bicker because they have nothing better to do. They are bored and need a challenge. If a stimulating environment is not provided for them, kids will create their own. What could be more exciting than to watch one's sister turn purple and scream with rage as one reads her diary aloud to the neighbors? What could possibly be more challenging than a good old-fashioned knock-down, drag-out fight, complete with sound and special effects?

Frustration

One mother told me that, as a child, she "picked on" her younger brothers out of a sense of rebellion. Her parents held a rather tight rein, so she was afraid to talk back or disobey them. But sensing their helplessness and lack of leadership whenever the children argued, she took advantage of their vulnerability.

The cause of sibling rivalry in any given family will be a complex patchwork of the above factors, as individual as the members of that family. For that reason, there are no pat answers. But neither is sibling rivalry an inevitable, hopeless situation from which there is no escape.

All of the aforementioned causes have one thing in common: they stem from universal needs that have not been adequately met. A child needs security, the knowledge that his home is stable and undergirded with love, and that each individual is important. He needs to feel good about himself. He needs love in all its manifestation— action, word and physical touch. The child needs "things to do," activities to stretch his mental, emotional, and spiritual "muscles," as well as the physical ones. And he needs limits—to give him confidence that someone cares about him. If any of these needs are ignored, or for some reason insufficiently met, a child will attempt substitute means of meeting them. He will use brothers and sisters as convenient targets for negative behavior, simply because they are so close at hand.

Recall my aphelandra plant and how hidden needs influence what is seen on the outside. Arguing, bickering, name-calling, tattling, and teasing are the visible *effects* of underlying problems. Too often we make the mistake of tackling them as problems in themselves.

The causes of conflicts between siblings usually can be distilled down to two main ones: (1) *Hostility*, which occurs when a child has physical or emotional needs which are not being completely met; and (2) *Personal differences*, those ideas, personality traits, and idiosyncracies that make each person unique from the next. Genuine sibling rivalry is in the first category. Many of the other disputes and problems that take place between children are not based on hatred, but rather on unchangeable differences between people. (It should be noted that if disagreements over personal differences become too heated, or too frequent, another need is being manifest—the need to learn how to disagree respectfully and to understand that we're all entitled to "be ourselves.")

Bill Gothard stresses that the roots behind every surface problem are *spiritual* in nature. Because a person's relationship to God affects his relationships with people, we cannot overlook the spiritual aspect. We must always be nurturing our own relationship with God if we want to have the greatest impact on our children. And they must be taught to rely on Him for wisdom and love when it comes to dealing with others.

I am encouraged by the final outcome of the story of Joseph. His jealous brothers hated him so much they had intended to kill him, but sold him instead to foreign slave traders.

In striking contrast to their attitude is Joseph's. He was so full of God's unconditional love that he provides a vivid portrait of the Christ to come. He was able to say, when providentially reunited with his brothers years later, "You intended to harm me, but God intended it for good to accomplish what is now being done, the saving of many lives. So then, don't be afraid. I will provide for you and your children." Then the Bible tells us that "he reassured them and spoke kindly to them" (Gen. 50:20, 21).

Now this man's attitude cannot be attributed to any factor in his home life, for during many of those years in Egypt, his home was a prison cell. But throughout his experience in Egypt, Joseph *knew* that he was enveloped and surrounded by God's love and care:

> The Lord greatly blessed Joseph there in the home of his master, so that everything he did succeeded (Gen. 39:2, TLB).

> The Lord blessed the household of the Egyptian because of Joseph (Gen. 39:5, NASB).

That same shroud of God's love exists for families today. Our children have an even better opportunity to learn of it than Joseph did, for they are enrolled in the most powerful learning institution God has created—the home. Parents can create the optimum atmosphere to help their children learn of God's unconditional, powerful love.

Parent Talk

1. Together, list some of the sibling problems each parent sees in your family. Discuss: What hidden needs might be at the root of these problems?
2. Discuss: How have we dealt with these problems in the past? Has this treatment been aimed at roots or fruit?
3. List several ways you can begin treating the roots more effectively.

Family Time

1. Using a Bible story book or your own rendition, retell the story of Joseph's life to your children. Ask them if they see causes behind the brothers' actions toward Joseph (boasting about his dream, his coat of many colors). As you are talking, stress that each child is important in your family and that you as parents try never to have a favorite child.
2. Ask each family member to tell about a time when he or she felt especially close to (or loving toward) a brother or sister. Parents may tell about experiences from their own youth or more recent years.

4

Environmental Control

During the Vietnam conflict, our friend Scott joined the Marines. When he reported for duty, he literally dropped out of our sight for thirteen weeks. We didn't hear a word from him although he was stationed only a few miles away from our home. He was just too busy training.

Later, as he described to us the regimen of physical activity and perfection of skills, we were amazed that all the men had come out sane and healthy. But they had made it, and they were stronger, more disciplined men as a result of the training.

Under the watchful eyes of a platoon sergeant and two drill instructors, the men worked out from dawn till bedtime. Their purpose: learning to kill, if need be, to defend the freedoms of others. It sounded gory, but as Scott reminded me, "You can't get out there in the heat of the battle and start having second thoughts about whether or not you belong there. We were disciplined, oriented, and scheduled to that end, right down to the last five minutes of the day."

Every facet of the recruits' training was preparing them for things they might experience after the training period was over. At such moments their reactions would have to be instantaneous; there would be no time to deliberate. The men practiced teamwork

37

through close-order drills, learning to march as a unit with precision and accuracy; through work parties, when an entire group would be responsible for getting a job done—and accountable if it wasn't done well enough. Team work was all-important. It would be unthinkable for them to get out on the battlefield and start bickering over whose order to follow.

Their training was physical (calisthenics, running, obstacle courses, and hand-to-hand combat), practical (rifle care, shooting skills, and survival techniques), and most of all, *mental.* It was, in a sense, programming. The men constantly read the Marine Corps handbook, memorizing general orders and procedures, thus learning how to respond automatically in crisis situations. They became Marines from the inside out. Today, some years later, he is a dedicated husband, father, and pastor; but I know that in his heart that man will always be one thing more—a Marine!

Our homes are "boot camps" of a sort, preparing children who are still tender and pliable for the rigors of survival in the battles of life. There is no need for the cold regimentation of a military atmosphere, but the concept behind that atmosphere is much the same: children, like soldiers, are largely a product of the environment in which they are trained. Our youngsters are gaining skills and experience that will prove valuable as they function in the adult world.

Siblings are an important part of this process—they certainly make up a large proportion of the environment! Through daily interaction and competition with a brother or sister, children learn acceptable ways of dealing with others. Within the seclusion of their home, free from the embarrassing looks or influence of outsiders, your children can learn to recognize emotions, both negative and positive, and discover ways of handling the feelings they have toward others. They can learn a sense of fair play. They can find out that, despite the infantile illusion that the sun rises and sets on their every whim, others exist too—others who have rights and deserve to be heard. They can learn what it is like not only to win but to lose, and how to work out problems with others. But it takes effort. And while it may seem like a lot of work to the children involved, it is even more work for the parents who are orchestrating the entire process.

We have just a few years with them, to help them form values, discover priorities, decide on a relationship with God. In this time we must also help them to know and accept themselves and to become what God wants them to be. And we must teach them to live responsibly in a world where they will not be coddled, and to get along with the people in that world. Considering the magnitude of those goals, the fact that we are dividing our efforts between more than one child, and the time lost through our inevitable mistakes, we need to utilize every moment of the years our children are in our care.

The goal of a military boot camp (training soldiers for war) and the goal of our home (training children for peace) seem to be polar opposites, yet they can be achieved in much the same manner. We must create the atmosphere that surrounds our children. This atmosphere will have a powerful effect on their lives and on many others. It is an atmosphere in which people "outdo each other in being helpful and kind to each other and in doing good" (Heb. 10:24, TLB).

So what will be the atmosphere of our miniature "boot camp"? It stands to reason that if our controlled environment focuses on fulfilling a child's needs (not wants), we will be eliminating potential causes of misbehavior. The next few chapters will be devoted to six "atmospheric conditions" which I consider essential for such an environment.

Parent Talk

1. Discuss: If a stranger had walked into our home 24 hours ago and was just now leaving, how would he describe our home's atmosphere? Would that be a fair analysis?
2. Discuss: What portions of our family's environment cause us to feel especially pleased? What areas could use improvement?

Family Time

1. Turn on a tape recorder and record an hour or two of activity when the family is in the house together. Play this back for the family a day later and evaluate what your home "sounds like."

2. Discuss: Why does God put people together in a family? Why doesn't He just let us all grow up individually—like trees or cabbages?
3. Why is living in our family good practice in getting along with people?

5

Acceptance: Blooming Where We're Planted

In many parts of the world, even today, people practice what we term, "marriage by arrangement." Parents and other doting relatives of the prospective bride and groom take care of the entire selection process and wedding festivities, leaving the young people to adjust to married life and to each other. These marriages are usually surprisingly durable.

I am glad, however, that I was born into a culture that allowed my husband and me to choose each other, so that we could initiate a relationship based on mutual love and admiration. I would think that partners in an arranged union might occasionally wonder, *Why did they match me up with this creep?*

These same sentiments may well reflect the plight of a young child when his territory is invaded by a crying baby. Mother and Dad, who *chose* each other, *chose* to have a family, and *chose* to love their first child, have *chosen* to have a new baby, and have *chosen* to love it, too! Poor Junior doesn't get to do any choosing; he can't select his parents, or any other family members who might happen along. He may have gone to bed one night secure in the knowledge that he was the central object of affection of the two people he most adored; but he was awakened the next morning by a beaming daddy who informed him that they have liked him so well they will soon bring home another child—and that Mommy will be gone in the meantime. Junior will be getting a roommate, someone with whom he has the dubious privilege of sharing not only his room, but his toys, his high chair, his grandparents, and his parents. He doesn't even know the little intruder yet, but he is having serious doubts as to whether or not this is all going to work out. It is no wonder many toddlers display less than unmitigated joy over their new siblings. In fact, given the circumstances and the emotional makeup of young children, it is probably remarkable that any get along well. Like the partners in an arranged marriage, children are often thrown into situations which they did not create or request.

The first step in making the situation as positive as possible is to build an atmosphere of *acceptance* in which the children feel and hear, "We belong together. God had a reason for putting us all in the same household. He knows we are good for each other, so let's *be* that!"

Some combinations of people are more compatible than others. As parents, we're bound to find out which are which very early in the game. We receive no guarantees that we will have no children whose personalities seem to clash from the very start. But it is possible, and necessary, to teach children to love each other as individuals, even if they find it hard to agree much of the time. This love first appears in the form of acceptance. And it will be hard to teach if we as parents are still working at learning it. Acceptance may seem to be a passive state of mind, but in truth, it often takes tremendous effort.

Many aspects of your family cannot be changed. No one can alter the fact that a person had a girl first and then a boy. No doctor can adjust the number of years or months that separate existing children. And a parent cannot erase a child's inherent personality and replace it with another. Neither can a parent erase mistakes of the past. Building an atmosphere of love in the home requires laying aside all the things which we cannot control. They must not matter to us anymore, for there is nothing we can do to change them.

Some parents feel that the greatest factor in sibling disputes and rivalry is this combination of unchangeable elements. Actually, these elements are few when compared to the things parents *can* control. With so many positive, concrete changes we *can* make, why waste time worrying over things beyond our power? It does help, however, to recognize these unchangeable factors. Acceptance seems to come more readily when we understand what makes it necessary.

Differences in Age

What is the ideal interval between children? As a childbirth instructor, I have heard them all, from "We want to have our kids ten months apart to get all the night feedings and diapers over with fast," to "Our daughter is eight and we think it's time for her to have a little brother or sister." I have also heard many other fantasies, such as "We're going to have a boy first, then a little girl," and "This is our *last* child." (Guess who was calling for a refresher course 13 months later?)

Various studies by countless experts have offered a multitude of theories on what the best spacing of children might be; the wise ones have concluded that there is no perfect age difference for siblings. The cold, hard fact is that we take them when we get them, and try to make the best of things.

In case you are still in the planning stages, however, or for those of you who are bewildered by your two-year-old's obstinate resistance to the altered family situation, here are some expert observations on age differences.

One authority tells us that an age difference of one or two years will create more conflicts than a wider age gap will.[5] The older child in such a pair often feels threatened, and the two become easy rivals for the attention and influence of the parents. Parents usually expend great effort to treat them "equally," sometimes unconsciously treating them as twins.

Another expert claims that children less than four years apart usually do well, with more problems occurring between four and six years. Children farther apart than six years are in "different worlds"; the younger viewing the elder more as a parent than as a peer.[6] Children of three to five who have never had to share the limelight may find it's a little tough moving over, but they are mature enough to be helpful, and when parents make the effort to talk about any problems, things usually work out acceptably.

One age span that seems especially difficult is an even two years apart. Yet many couples, who have the option of planning these things out, deliberately choose this spacing for their children. It probably stems from the fact that a child of 12-15 months is extremely cute, but not quite a "baby" anymore. Mom and Dad, pleased with their track record thus far, sit back radiantly and say, "Isn't she getting big? She's going to need a brother or sister pretty soon." They take appropriate action, pass the pregnancy test, and WHAM—around 18-20 months, Junior enters the "terrible twos."

Regardless of whether or not we consider this period of time to be *that* terrible, it is a very trying phase for most children—a kind of adolescence between infancy and childhood that lasts for about 12 months. At times the toddler feels small and helpless and wants to be treated as such. Throwing a new baby into that volatile emotional situation is like lighting a match to check a gas tank. It can mean trouble for even the hardiest of families. Most of the desperate tales of sibling incompatibility have come to me from parents of children 1 ½ to 2 ½ years apart.

Boys vs. Girls

The children's gender can make a great difference, as well. Scientists are now proving that there actually are basic, biological differences that make boys act one way and girls another.

Mothers observe that a good deal of their daughters' viciousness is verbal. Cattiness and sniping with a sharp tongue are tactics girls seem to master well at an early age. Boys tend to be more physical about their differences; they'd rather swing it out. Neither way is preferable, but if we are aware of these tendencies, we can watch for these patterns to emerge. Do we have rules in our homes banning physical injury, but none governing assaults with words? The verbal kind can often cause more long-term pain and damage.

Girls can work up a bowlful of tears over very little, while many boys would be too ashamed to cry over much greater hurts. So, if a sweet, angelic daughter comes running teary-eyed to report that her brother slugged her, there's a good likelihood that he had a reason —has she coyly (and covertly) been teasing him to the point of explosion? We must make sure we're getting the entire story.

Children of the same sex may be more intimate because they share a room and some similar interests. However, these same factors may also lead to hot competition between the two. We cannot assume, just because our children are the same sex, that they will be close, or even that they will *want* to be.

Since girls often mature faster, physically and emotionally, than boys, we can expect a good deal of contention (especially in the adolescent years) if the daughter is close in age to her brother. There may be times when she feels and acts much older than he, and where he is mistaken for the "little" brother. This is likely to bruise his ego and fan the flames of jealousy. We can be aware of this and try to ward it off before it happens. It may help to talk with one's daughter about this, when she is in a receptive mood, and point out how bad a person can feel when not given the respect he is hoping for and deserves. You might say, "I'm sure Mike feels embarrassed that he isn't as tall as you are. I hope you'll be considerate of his feelings and not make a big issue out of it. I really appreciate the fact that you're mature enough for us to discuss this on an adult level."

It is better to arrange these little discussions so they take place in a "cool" moment, removed from the fever of argument. Ideas are less likely to "sink in" if they are thrust forth in a tone of irritated preaching.

Temperaments

Every child is as unique as a snowflake. Each baby, at the moment of conception, has within those two joining cells his life's potential. He will have ideas and abilities, likes and dislikes, which at first are unknown to his parents. Will he be an athlete or a spectator? An eager beaver or a pokey pup? Will he be funny or serious? What will be his favorite food? Will he be a morning lark or a night owl? Will he be artistic and introspective, or buoyant and extroverted? Will he be President? Will he find a cure for cancer? Will he have children of his own? Will he be a *she*?

When a baby is born, no one knows much about him—except God, who sees all of us, inside and out, while we are still in the womb (Ps. 139:16; Jer. 1:5). Every member of a family unit has been placed there by God for a purpose. Only He understands the delicate intricacies that make up each complex personality. Only He knows what will best help each one of us to grow and mature into the person He wants.

These variations can be illustrated by the differing qualities of modeling compounds. One of our sons' favorite pastimes is molding and shaping Pla-doh®. This product is soft and malleable, but hardens when left exposed to the air. Oil-base modeling clay *looks* slightly more difficult to manipulate when cold, yet never completely hardens. Both substances can be shaped in the same manner, however. The clay a potter uses would have different traits from either of the above, but it too is similar, in that it can be formed according to the tastes of the artist. Other materials, such as concrete, putty and plaster, all have the potential of being molded into something beautiful, but a craftsman working with all or several of these substances must keep in mind their individual properties.

The same can be said of our children. There are many areas of their lives we can guide, bend, shape, and prune, but we cannot change the properties of the basic material from which a child has been created. This material is his temperament.

A person can be classified in a variety of ways: introvert/extrovert, positive/negative, leader/follower, strong-willed/compliant, optimist/pessimist. One who knows Christ may also partake of an abundance of spiritual gifts, which enhance his personality the way oil enhances the beauty in a piece of fine wood.

Our family has especially benefited from explanations of the four basic human temperaments and their twelve combinations, most recently explained by Tim and Beverly LaHaye. As we stated in *The Natural Childbirth Book*, it is a practical and easily applied psychology. And it is highly profitable for every parent to have a working knowledge of basic personality types so he can apply it as he assumes the roles of counselor, referee, arbitrator, diplomat, and mediator.

The temperament theory supposes that each of us has one predominant temperament, combined with a lesser degree of another of the four. Each temperament has its own characteristic set of strengths and weaknesses. A person with a "good" personality is one who has learned, with God's guidance, to overcome his weaknesses and maximize his strengths to their fullest potential. This should be our goal for our children. Here, then, is a brief look at each of the four temperaments:

Sanguine: This is perhaps the most easily recognized of all the temperaments. The sanguine person is happy, vivacious, generous, outgoing, warm and friendly. He loves to participate in everything and won't be found on the sidelines unless both legs are broken. He has a few potential weaknesses, of course: disorganized, undisciplined, easily swayed, and somewhat undependable. The sanguine person has many good ideas and loads of enthusiasm, but he has difficulty actually getting things accomplished. Such a child is frequently "most popular," often loud and funny, and *always* with other people. As an adult he may be a good salesman, entertainer, speaker, or professional athlete. He thrives in the limelight.

Choleric: A choleric individual is self-disciplined, optimistic, confident and determined. He is a "go-getter," an achiever. This person works almost compulsively and can be counted on to get things done. In the process, however, negative traits such as coldheartedness, impatience, anger, and a short temper may reveal themselves. A choleric child will be diligent and reliable, his biggest problem being that of anger. As an adult, a choleric may be found in a position of leadership, such as foreman, administrator, independent businessman, or military leader.

Melancholic: The melancholic person is generally more introverted, more reserved than either of the preceding types. He tends to be sensitive to others, analytical, practical, artistic, dependable, meticulous, and self-sacrificing. He is a loyal friend. The weaknesses of this temperament include excessive worry and doubt, a critical spirit, pessimism, self-centeredness, easily hurt feelings, and moodiness. As a child, such a person is often shy and prefers indoor, creative activities to outdoor group play. A melancholic makes an excellent teacher because he usually exhibits unlimited patience. He also may be a musician, artist, or craftsman.

Phlegmatic: This is perhaps the "coolest" of all the temperaments. The phlegmatic person is usually quiet and reserved, easygoing, and provides enjoyable company. He is careful and practical, almost overly cautious. His dry sense of humor is often a great source of entertainment to those who stop to listen, but he won't flaunt it. On the negative side, he can be slow, unmotivated, and passive. He may also be a tease, as he has a tendency to make fun of the weaknesses displayed in other temperaments. A phlegmatic child will be calm, relaxed, compliant, and somewhat reserved—a definite spectator. As an adult, a phlegmatic may make a good teacher, diplomat, or accountant. He almost always works for somebody else, rather than running his own business.

As stated earlier, no one's personality consists of just one temperament. Because most of us are a combination of two, each individual possesses a unique balance of strengths and weaknesses. A person who has his weaknesses under control and is utilizing his strengths will be a well-adjusted person, regardless of his temperament.

God has made each of us the way we are, totally different from any other person. Therefore He has a special plan for each person's unique combination of attributes.

Your child's temperament can begin to reveal itself at a very early age. You can exert tremendous influence on many of your child's ideas, preferences, and attitudes, but you cannot change the underlying temperament. As a parent you can expect that, just as there are some people you like better than others, your child will probably have "people preferences." Certain personalities blend quite well, while others clash noisily every time they are within shouting distance. Most, however, can *learn* to get along. You can foster in your home such an attitude of individual acceptance and respect of differences. Much of this will depend on your acceptance of the situation and how you verbalize it.

One authority recommends that children be *taught* what their personal strengths and weaknesses are, and shown how these affect the rest of the family. This might be a good idea, but a parent must be extremely careful not to "label" a child in such a way that the child feels locked into a certain pattern of behavior. Some parents will say to a babysitter, right in front of their child, "She's shy; she'll cry when we leave." Their daughter, feeling compelled to prove the accuracy of her parents' assessment, cries. A parent should, instead, help his child to know and accept himself and others in a constructive manner. Here is an example:

Our oldest son is a combination of sanguine and phlegmatic; confident, and carefree, he is a happy-go-lucky fellow who is easy to live with and provides a laugh a minute. The second is serious-minded, determined, and imaginative—probably a choleric-melancholic. They are a good combination—one entertainer, one spectator; one leader, one follower. They get along well about 98% of the time. Occasionally, however, as Sanguine is playing, making faces, telling jokes, and teasing (in hopes of evoking a laugh), he manages to spark his brother's short fuse—his desire to be left alone. Ever since we discovered the potential for such trouble, we have been coaching them (each privately).

To our sanguine we say the following: "God made you very special in that you always seem able to make a good time out of anything that happens. That's a very special gift, and people like to be around you. But most people sometimes feel like being alone, thinking about things instead of talking or playing. Your brother is not just like you, but we need different kinds of people in the world. At times he may not feel as cheerful as you. When you notice this, it's best to leave him alone until he decides he wants to play. Can you think of some things you can do by yourself at such a time?"

We are also teaching the other child, whose choleric nature allows little tolerance for the whims of others. We'll say such things as,

"Don't be mad at your brother. He likes you so much he wants to play with you a great deal. He was just trying to have fun. Can you tell him nicely, 'No thank you, I don't feel like being funny right now'?" Usually he will comply to that degree, and has been known on several occasions to actually become jovial once he was given the freedom to be "himself."

We cannot alter the love of fun and games one has, nor can we force his brother to be amused by them. But we can train each to respect the other's differences. We can teach Sanguine not to tease people who do not respond with laughter. And we can teach Choleric that it is not acceptable to go on a rampage just because he doesn't like someone's face. Such lessons will help them not only now, but also in their future relationships with others.

You must gauge what you say to your children according to their temperaments, their moods at the time, and their understanding of what it all means. One child may not be old enough to understand terms such as "personality" or "choleric," but from the time he can understand anything at all, you can begin implanting an attitude of respect for the preferences of others.

Here are some examples of dealing with these matters:

"Some people, like you and I, could talk all the time and never get tired of it. Others, like Daddy and Justin, sometimes need quiet. Let's try and be quiet for them, okay?"

Applying these techniques directly to siblings and their spats, you might try, "Jessica, some people enjoy being the boss and making all the rules, trying to have everything go their way. This seems to be the way Michelle is. Just remember that you don't *have* to be bossed around by Michelle. But if you don't like something she wants to do, what could you say to her?"

To Michelle you might say, "You are a very good leader, and I think that you have a special talent for organizing people and thinking up good ideas. But you must remember that other people sometimes have good ideas too. It's fun to be the boss sometimes, but you need to let Jessica practice making some decisions. How could you let her do that?"

Here's another situation: "Jeff, I'm proud that you made the soccer team and that you are so coordinated and strong. It's a special gift God has given you. But sometimes Steven's feelings are hurt when people talk about how athletic you are and ask him why he doesn't play soccer. We know that he likes snakes and bugs and microscopes and things like that, but it's something he does mostly in private. Would you help us make Steven feel good about what he does well? Can you think of any ways we could encourage him?"

To Steven you might say, "Isn't it great how God has given each of us a different set of interests and abilities? I have never known an eight-year-old who knows so much about various insects."

Be careful not to mention a child's negative traits, except in the light of the positive. Don't say, "You sure are scatterbrained. We're going to have to work on that." Instead, be tactful and say something like, "A person who is as friendly as you are and so excited about life can get so busy that he forgets to finish things he has started. We need to really concentrate on remembering what we're doing and finishing it up because it's easy to get distracted—isn't it?"

The Family Totem Pole

Besides temperament, other factors bear a strong influence on how the children in a family treat one another. Birth order, for instance, seems to be a significant factor. The traits of a classic first-born, middle child, or "baby," when combined with an already-unique personality, provide a slight twist, like the gentle nudging of a kaleidoscope, which produces an entirely different array of color and design.

Bradford Wilson, a researcher of birth order, says, "Children grow up in quite different environments depending on whether they are oldest, youngest, or in the middle, because of, among other things, their mother and father's changing economic status and increasing experience as parents. . . . Power struggles and jealousies between siblings are often dictated by their positioning."[7] While three children may grow up in the same family, the family surrounding each child is not the same at all. Parents have a lot of time and energy to direct toward their first child. By the time the third or fourth arrives, they are older, more involved in the world around them, and may be flagging just a bit (perhaps "ready to drop from exhaustion" would be a better term). One child may be the oldest sister of two younger brothers, while the youngest may consider himself the kid brother of two teenagers. Also, one child may have arrived in the midst of marital or financial problems, which caused one or both parents to be, indeed, "different."

A firstborn child is, for a time, the only child of two people who probably are still committed to one another and to the idea of a family. What they may lack materially they compensate for with an abundance of happy moments together. Parents are eager to do a good job with their first child. They tend to heap praise on the little prodigy every time he does something right. This child usually continues to be quite confident and may be a good leader and achiever. Of the 39 men who have been President, 25 were "oldest" children, either by virtue of being born first, by being the oldest surviving child, by being the oldest son, or by being the first child of a "second family."[8] The oldest child may take a parental attitude toward younger children, which the siblings may or may not resent. He may set a shining example which his siblings cannot escape. Even years later when *they* enter kindergarten, or junior high, or college, they may encounter such questions as, "Aren't you Judy's little sister? Boy, she was the sharpest math student we ever had here!" The oldest child may flaunt the privileges which he obtained by being there first. As the oldest of three girls myself, I admit that the possibilities for creative power-displays are infinite!

Dr. Philip Very, another birth-order expert, says, "Think about what happens when the first baby comes along. There are months of preparation. New clothes. New baby furniture. There is a savings bond. Probably a mint coin set. A baby shower. (Only the first baby, remember, gets a baby shower.) And the photographs—hundreds, right?

"The second child gets what? Hand-me-downs. No savings bond. No coin set. No shower. And in all the photographs he's standing next to his older and taller brother or sister.

"By the time the third child comes along, forget it! He's lucky if he gets in one photograph, peeking between the legs of his older brother and sister."[9]

In keeping with Dr. Very's observations, more research has been done and more information is available on firstborns than on subsequent children.

A second-born child probably doesn't resent the hand-me-downs because he is more congenial—or because he has developed this congeniality as a defense mechanism against the stigma of hand-me-downs. This person makes a lot of friends, usually sticking closer to peers than to family. He may have a competitive streak, which he uses to compensate for not being biggest and oldest. Our second-born son competes very effectively with his brother, who has a three-year edge on him. He insists on trying (and usually does quite well at) everything his brother does. He holds out doggedly for his "fair share," and he usually gets it. How has he gotten away with this? Because, until recently, he has also been the "baby"!

The baby of the family, or the last-born, takes advantage of this position to hold his own. He cannot win by size, or strength, or knowledge, so he resorts to a cunning charm. When my sisters and I were young, anytime we *really* wanted anything, we sent Sheryl to ask Dad. Her big brown eyes and winsome manner had an appeal that we exploited whenever we wanted to go out for dinner or needed money for something our parents might deem "frivolous." The last-born child is often more quiet and introspective, and some believe he has a greater interest in things of a spiritual nature.

The positions and relationships of children in a family are complex, and experts sometimes liken them to the configurations of stars in the heavens—therefore referring to them as constellations. There may be several such constellations in which your children are members. If they are frequently exposed to cousins, neighbors, or children you babysit, a pecking order will usually emerge and you will notice each child behaving very predictably toward each other child. If his time with these "second siblings" is frequent, this pecking order may have a greater effect on a child than his actual birth order.

Life in the Rock Tumbler

Our sons, like many boys, have shown a keen interest in rocks of all shapes and sizes (their "collections" are kept near my washing machine, where, on a daily basis, I pluck pebbles from pockets). One day we visited a rock shop, and the boys were enamored by a large barrel filled with shiny, smooth, richly-colored stones. It felt good to reach a hand deep among the cool, smooth rocks and come up with something lovely enough to use as jewelry. The boys, of course, wanted to know where all those gorgeous stones had been "found."

A sales clerk then explained that the rocks are just ordinary ones like those the boys stuff in their pockets. They then are placed with abrasive compounds in a tumbler that resembles a large cookie jar lying on its side. The tumbler rotates briskly for some days, causing the rocks to roll and pound against each other. The rough edges are slowly ground away in this process, and the final product is a batch of shiny, decorative stones (that can be sold for up to 50¢ each!).

It occurred to me that our homes are much like that machine. We *all* have rough edges that need smoothing out. The very presence of other temperaments—rough edges—is often the thing that enhances our spiritual growth. The process is not always totally comfortable, but the end result is a wonderful product.

One of our most important tasks as parents is to help our children accept life's inevitable polishings, and in so doing develop a greater acceptance of others. Once our children are able to cope with unchangeable factors, we can help them tackle those things which can be controlled.

Parent Talk

1. Discuss: What are some problem areas in our family that we cannot change?
2. Discuss: How can we as parents minimize the ill-effects of these unchangeables on the children who face them?

Family Time

1. On a sheet of paper or poster board, list (as a family) all the good qualities you can think of about each member. Focus especially on traits that make each person different from the others.
2. Discuss:
   a. How can these traits be helpful to this person throughout life?
   b. Why is this person good for our family?
   c. How could these qualities be even better developed?
   d. Are there any qualities we *should* have, but don't?
   e. How can we acquire these qualities?

6

Parental Example: Super Soil

One cool Saturday morning in late autumn, a phone call came for my husband while he was outside working on the car. I therefore took a message and promised to relay it to him. Our pajama-clad sons were absorbed in play, so I decided to slip out quickly before they had a chance to miss or follow me. As I leaned over the car's engine, chatting with the back of Ralph's head, Jonathan came wandering out—barefoot.

I frowned at him, and said, "What are you doing out here with no shoes on? Go back inside—I'll be in soon."

He stared at me in confusion and replied, with all the indignation a two-year-old can muster, "Well, you don't have *your* shoeses on, neither." I looked down at my feet. Oops.

At another time I was lying down with Jonny waiting for him to fall asleep. Our pillow talk went something like this:

"Mommy, are your teeth sharp?"

"Yes. And do you know why God gives us sharp teeth?"

"Uh-huh. For biting into our food."

"That's right. Good night."

A long pause followed. "And for taking off your fingernails, huh, Mom?"

57

Every day of their growing-up years (with the possible exception of the teen years) our children say such things as, "Look, Mom! When I stand on this chair I'm as big as you!" or "I want to be a 'destruction worker' just like my dad," or "May I wear makeup like you, Mom?" or "May we stay up as late as you do?" or "I wish I had some boots like Daddy's." They serve as continuous, gentle reminders that our children are observing us and they want to do what we do. This is how they learn.

Albert Schweitzer once said, "There are only three ways to teach a child. The first is by example. The second is by example. The third is by example."[10]

Have you ever sat with friends, watching your children playing together, and commented, "He's just like his dad . . . "? It's almost eerie to see in one's own child a mirror image of one's own traits, quirks, and interests. Many times I have rolled my eyes and said to someone, or to no one in particular, "He's *so* stubborn—he's the original 'strong-willed child,' " knowing full well that any child of mine who happens to be a trifle stubborn certainly comes by it honestly (from me). In fact, most of *us* are more like our parents than we are prepared to admit.

Consider your parents as you remember them from your childhood, when they were about the age you are now. Do you recall any likenesses between them and yourself? I am constantly saying things to our boys and simultaneously "hearing" my mother say them to me in my memory. Observe any brothers and sisters you have, and notice "family traits" that you all share. There are bound to be some, even if they are not instantly noticeable.

The training and values my parents provided me could not have been taught effectively in any other way. And one thing has become increasingly clear as the years go by: children pick up most of their cues from their parents. Ours are now looking to us to *show* them (not just tell them) what is good and acceptable behavior. Perhaps this explains why half the sons and 10% of the daughters in families where both parents are alcoholics are likely to become alcohol-dependent. And why most child abusers were themselves abused as children. The Bible tells us that the sins of a father can affect three and four generations (Num. 14:18). Guess who perpetuates the effect!

An interesting example of the parent-to-child influence is the family of Abraham. Abraham's great-grandchildren, the brothers of Joseph, were probably "justified" in their jealousy toward Joseph (who seems to have opened his mouth a few times too many). After all, their father, Jacob, had visibly played favorites, and showered only one of his twelve sons with extra affection and lavish gifts. But of course, Jacob didn't know any better. His father, Isaac, had made it obvious that he, too, had a favorite—and it wasn't Jacob. If we take one more step back, we see that Isaac had felt the squeeze of sibling competition (with his half-brother, Ishmael) and that his father, Abraham, had visibly favored him. The persistent jealousy in this family bears out the truth of the statement in Numbers 14.

If there are still skeptics who doubt that parental example is a major factor in children's behavior, I invite you to consider two separate families:

The first family was given a pseudonym by the researchers who compiled its history. This was to protect the members of the family who did not happen to have criminal records and wished to protect their reputations. These people were all descendants of a man who was often unemployed, drank heavily, and frequented brothels. Two of his sons married two of his five illegitimate daughters, producing at least six generations of crime and pauperism that has fascinated criminologists for years. The mother of some of these children was affectionately known in her town as "Margaret, mother of criminals." Of over 700 descendants traced, we find 84 prostitutes; 82 illegitimate children; 191 arrested for crimes such as burglary, larceny, forgery, and robbery; 20 murderers; 15 rapists; and 7 arsonists. Over 280 were considered paupers, dependent on public or private charity for their support.[11]

In contrast are 400 descendants of the famous preacher, Jonathan Edwards, which have been traced. Besides the fact that Edwards himself was the son and grandson of preachers, at least 100 of his progeny have become ministers, missionaries, and theology instructors. Fourteen were college presidents, and 100 became college professors. More than a hundred became lawyers and judges, sixty became physicians, and many more were authors, editors, or prominent leaders in American industry.[12] Parental example *is* important!

Children are more impressed with action than they are with talk. In a given day, we may get in five minutes of actual "moralizing" (and we can waste that, if it's not done in the right spirit). Our children do get, however, a 24-hour "sermon" from us every day, whether we plan it or not. They learn what things in life are most important to us by which things they see us do first and with the most urgency. They learn how to deal with frustration by watching us in a traffic jam, or when the dinner is inadvertently cremated. They learn hospitality and charity from the way we treat people—even their noisy, and sometimes sticky, little friends. They learn the role of "self" by seeing our selfishness or lack of it. They make as much room for God in their lives as they see us make for Him in ours.

Here are a few ways by which we can improve the example we give our children:

1. *Limit our own fighting.* If children see their parents quibble and bicker over every little thing from who takes out the trash to what brand of soap to have in the shower, they are going to get the impression that quarreling is a necessary part of life and the wisest course of action. If, on the other hand, they see us respond to those with whom we disagree in love, displaying patience, tolerance, and selflessness, they will adopt these actions and attitudes as their own.

2. *Be pleasant and cheerful as much as possible.* It's not easy to maintain a smile when everything around seems to be dissolving. One year, as the construction industry went into a tailspin leaving my husband with about three months of no work (and no pay), almost every mechanical thing we owned malfunctioned. Both cars required major repairs, our water heater had to be replaced, the plumbing needed extensive work, and three major appliances broke down. I think I was crabby and grumpy about 90% of the time. In the wake of my ungrateful spirit, our sons became equally ornery.

A day can be wonderful if it is begun with a smile and a cheerful outlook. This comes naturally to one of our sons, who can bound out of bed at 5:00 a.m. and be smiling before his feet hit the floor.

The other, however, is a "slow warmer," taking a half hour or so to get his eyes open. We began noticing that our responses to them were as predictable as the boy's wake-up habits. We would greet "Mr. Sunshine" with big smiles and cheerful chatter; but when his brother awoke, we would voice a wary "Hi" and keep our distance—as if afraid he would snap our heads off! However, when we began greeting him with a cheery, "Hi, Buddy, you look like you had a good rest," he began getting up in better spirits. Our behavior had been setting the tone for his attitude.

3. *Don't do things they aren't allowed to do.* A parent is often tempted, when angry, to hit a child (or spank, swat, slap, etc.). If a child has done something that has made us mad, a good rule to follow is, "If you *feel* like hitting him, *don't*." Time to cool off should precede disciplinary measures. A child, even a very young one, can tell the difference between an angry swat and one given in love as a learning tool. I have never seen a child who habitually hit others when angry that was not treated that same way by someone older and influential in his life (a parent, relative, or babysitter). Physical discipline is appropriate only when the parent can honestly say, "This hurts me more than it hurts you."

I believe name-calling is the most injurious of all forms of sibling abuse. It rarely leaves physical scars, but the emotional injuries left by a few well-chosen words from a sharp-tongued whippersnapper can persist for life. Many parents are no more gracious in their remarks. On several occasions I have heard parents use name-calling against their children, and it always hurts the child and me. Name-calling can be practiced *absente reo* (the defendant being absent) with expressions such as, "That was really stupid of him," or "What a jerk ... nerd ... turkey ... clod ... clown ... klutz ... buzzard ..." This is "adult" name-calling. Parents can be very adept at this from behind the wheel of a car. We then wonder what would possibly prompt one of our children to call the other "dummy."

4. *Speak positively of other people.* If Mom acts friendly to her "friends," then comes home and verbally tears them to shreds, a child will develop a warped sense of what true friendship is. If Daddy is a Sunday school teacher, but the traditional Sunday dinner

fare is "broiled preacher," a child will have a hard time understanding loyalty and patience.

5. *Be conscious of tone of voice.* The first time one of our sons (the one who *never* gets mad) shouted at me irritably, he said, "Will you *wait* a minute?" He was barely two at the time, and I was stunned by his outburst. But not for long. As I reflected on the past few weeks I realized that his newly-acquired talkativeness had nearly driven me batty, and on several occasions I had put him off with those same words—and the same tone of voice—while I finished writing a letter, reading a chapter, or making a phone call.

A mother wrote to me, "The more loving [my husband and I] are to one another and the boys, the easier they are to take care of and the better they seem to get along. If I am in a bad mood or 'less than patient' with them, they are less than patient with one another. It seems to be a vicious circle."

6. *Stress teamwork by being a part of the "team."* Uphold each other's decisions and each other. Support your children. Let them know that no matter what happens, you'll always keep their highest good in mind. Stress to each child frequently the value of his or her brothers and sisters. Point out ways that they are good for one another, and remind him of things they like to do together. Build their loyalty toward one another from the start through family loyalty. If your example shows them that the family and the feelings of each member are important to you, this will elevate their concept of the family as a "team."

7. *Create happy family memories.* Give your children the idea that family members can be as fun and as good friends as anyone else. The number of enjoyable moments should be greater than the unpleasant times. Plan family activities and outings, and as you do them, comment, "This is fun. We really have a good time when we're together," or "I'd rather be with you guys on this fishing trip than anywhere else in the world," or "I'd rather spend the day with you than be a millionaire," or "I'm glad we can have such a good time even just staying here at home, as long as we're together!"

Jesus said, "Love one another as I have loved you," but He also *showed* us how. If we desire to see godly behavior in our children, it is imperative that we show them what they should be like. When children can see in their parents an example worth imitating, they have learned from the most effective teachers in all the world. Keep the same attitude Paul had—"And the Lord make you to increase and abound in love one toward another, and toward all men, even *as we do* toward you" (1 Thess. 3:12, KJV).

Parent Talk

1. List five ways in which you are similar to your own parents.
2. Comment on traits you see in your spouse that seem to have been acquired from parents (keep this discussion positive!).
3. Discuss: What are some of the mannerisms and expressions our children use that they seem to have gotten from us?

Family Time

1. Get out photo albums, scrapbooks, and baby books and stroll together down Memory Lane. Let each person express his feelings about these recorded events.
2. Discuss:
   a. What was the most enjoyable vacation we ever took?
   b. Was there ever a time when you were really excited about doing something as a family?
   c. Think of different people's homes we've visited. What did you notice was different about the homes you liked the most?
   d. Do you remember your first day of kindergarten? What was the best thing about that day?

7

Self-esteem:
Strengthening the Stem

"Mom, whom do you love most—Jonny or me?"

What parent hasn't been asked that question, or worse yet, been accused of having a favorite among the clan? Everyone wants to be on top. A young man is not content just to be a good ball player; he wants to be on a pro team to really be impressive. And if he makes it that far, he has to be on the team that wins the World Series. And if he can make it to the series, he would like to score the tie-breaking run in the bottom of the tenth. Nice, but not too likely.

For every man who makes it to the World Series, there are tens of thousands who *don't* make it. Who are they? At the moment the winning run is scored, it doesn't much matter who they are; they are not the *best*. The world trains its eyes on the "est" of everything— fastest, smartest, richest, strongest. Those who are not the best, or "est," often go unnoticed, and presumably are unimportant.

Children yearn for reassurance of their importance and value. When this assurance is lacking, trouble often crops up between brothers and sisters. They may then begin watching for one or both parents to show even the slightest sign of favoritism in order to pounce with accusations. Also, when feeling unsure of their status in the family, they may invent conflicts and disagreements for the specific purpose of pushing the parent to take someone's side. Misunderstandings, resentment, and a fair amount of noise are the end result. Feelings of failure and frustration are the parents' portion.

It is unlikely that any family can fully avoid problems of this sort, but there are ways to reduce them. How? By helping each child to see himself as valuable and worthwhile, an important member of a team on which there is *no* "most valuable player." A sense of security can be built into a child beginning in earliest infancy. This is accomplished by the following:

1) *Focused, personal attention* for each child, with special consideration given to meeting the individual's unique needs.

2) Showing a genuine interest in each child by maintaining *open lines of communication.*

3) Surrounding each child with *encouraging words*—positive affirmations that promote good feelings about himself and his importance to the family.

Focused Attention

It's very easy to give attention to a baby. Not only are his eyes, chubby cheeks, and velvety skin irresistible, but his needs are simple and easily met. When he is hungry we offer food. If he's wet, we change his diaper. When he wants to be close to us we hold him. When he cries we answer. I personally have no problem showering a baby with tons of love and attention. We show a baby his importance to us by being present, responding promptly, and meeting his needs—the same way our Father demonstrates His care for us.

Toddlers, by their very nature, demand our attention. (If you don't believe it, try leaving a two-year-old alone in any room of the house for ten minutes—or even five!) A toddler's presence defies ignoring. His needs are expressed differently than a baby's, but are no less important.

There are two main reasons why a child requires so much care and attention in the early years. The first, and most obvious, is to insure he gets what is needed for healthy development. The second, and less obvious, is to help the inexperienced parents form habits of involvement with the child. The dependency of childhood is our Creator's way of making sure *we* don't shirk our parental duties.

As a child grows, his behavior changes. An eight-year-old, instead of wailing for his supper, will *say* he is hungry. If hot, instead of crying about it, he will change clothes. His emotional responses change too. At every stage he needs to be touched, hugged, cuddled and caressed, but he may be less open about his need. He may become reluctant to bare joys or heartaches, but he still longs to know his parents do care about those things.

We parents must stay a step ahead of this process, devising ways to meet our children's need for attention *before* they feel deprived. The alternative, of course, is to let the kids devise their ways of getting our attention, usually through misbehavior. Many times quarrels and squabbles between siblings are someone's way of saying, "Hey, Mom and Dad, please notice me!"

It takes less effort to prevent this kind of behavior than to correct it, but sometimes we parents forget. Or we misunderstand our children's needs. One mother observed that her oldest daughter had never seemed very cuddly or affectionate, and that she was becoming very aggressive and hostile toward her younger sister and brother. This mother concluded, probably correctly, that "just because a child isn't cuddly by nature doesn't mean she doesn't need touch. But it's up to the parents to find ways of meeting the needs that are suited to the child's personality. With Sarah, this entails games, tickle fights, fussing with her clothes and hair, helping her learn gymnastics and stunts. A quick, unexpected hug at times has also worked quite well."

One of our sons was of the touch-me-not genre. Or so we thought. We later concluded that, like almost everyone, he really does like to be touched, but not confined. Ralph solves this by doing a lot of tickling, swinging, and rough-housing with our two boys. (You can imagine what our house looks like.) I approach the matter by playing little games to get the boys close to me. Sometimes I sit on the couch with an exaggerated pout, waiting for one of them to ask,

"What's wrong?" I reply, "I guess I just need a hug." He usually complies. If not, I then say teasingly, "But don't *you* hug me. . . ." That line always works. Sometimes I will entrap one of them by asking, "Will you please bring me that pen?" When he gets close to me I grab him and wrestle him to the floor with hugs and kisses, both of us laughing all the way.

Ralph and I take advantage of every opportunity to hold our little ones close, for we know that too soon the day will come when they might say, "Aw, Mom, not now." We enjoy their crawling into our bed and warming their feet on our backs. Someday they won't want to.

We believe parents should follow their parental urges, and hold and caress their children frequently. Don't, therefore, make yours misbehave before you answer their cries for help or companionship. Let your children be near you as much as possible; smile at them and talk to them frequently. No one (even a baby) was ever spoiled by too much affection. (What kind of fireworks would go off if your spouse told you he was going to ignore you for a while so you wouldn't get "spoiled"?)

As you show your child loving attention, he will be able to see in you that "love is patient, love is kind. It does not envy, it does not boast, it is not proud. It is not rude, it is not self-seeking, it is not easily angered, it keeps no record of wrongs. Love does not delight in evil, but rejoices with the truth. It always protects, always trusts, always hopes, always perseveres. Love never fails" (1 Cor. 13:4-8). He will know that your love for him is firm and unfailing. From your example, he will learn to love others in the same way.

Communication

A child's cries as a baby and the parent's responses to them are the beginning of an important process that hopefully will last a lifetime. The growth of communication will help the child to see his parent as wise and concerned.

Most of us, if asked to define "communication," would immediately think of the "noisemaking" aspect—talk. But while making yourself heard is an important part of clear communication, I would like to suggest a more significant and often overlooked factor: the *listener.*

Why do we feel so foolish if we are caught talking to ourselves? Because no one is listening! A radio station has absolutely no purpose in broadcasting if no one tunes in to listen. A television program that receives low Nielsen ratings doesn't last long. A person can babble into a CB transmitter all day, but if no one pays attention to his receiver, there is no communication. At least half of the process of oral communication is listening.

Most of us have no trouble in the talking department, especially when dealing with our children. It is important to talk to them, to explain things, to impart ideas and knowledge, to show that they're worth talking to. But many times as parents we fall into the trap of believing that we are the only people who could possibly have anything significant to say.

Have you ever listened to yourself when you're on the phone with an especially verbose person on the other end? My husband has made fun of me at times for the endless string of absent-minded "uh-huhs" and "reallys." Sometimes I sound the same when the children come bounding in with their breathless chatter. But it is important to listen to them rather than dominating household conversation with "important" matters. They should be allowed to speak freely and know they are being heard. A parent's listening attitude can seem to speak far louder than spoken words when it comes to transferring values and ideals.

As we take a genuine interest in what our children say, we convey a message to them more clearly than if we used a billboard and two megaphones, announcing, "You are important. You are worthwhile. I care about you as much as any mother or dad could care about a child."

Counselors, and other people whose business depends on dialogue, use a technique called "active listening." I define it as the "tape recorder technique." When I was teaching Lamaze classes in our home, I would record each session and lend the tape to students who had been absent or to our teacher trainees. Before a class began, I would set up the machine and say into the microphone, "Testing, one, two, three." Then I would rewind, and play it back, to make sure what I had said had been picked up. If the recorder was unreliable (I went through four in five years), during the class break I would play it back again, just to make sure nothing was being lost. And of course, after class, I'd run fast forward through the tape, stopping occasionally to check the recording. The more often I got the results I wanted, the more confidence I had, not only in the machine, but in my teaching methods. I was assured the students were receiving the information in a way they could understand and that those who listened to the tape would get what they needed also.

Active listening gives the one doing the talking confidence that he has been heard and understood correctly. When listening actively, the hearer "plays back" to the speaker another version of what has just been said. He tries to mirror that person's feelings as well as the facts that are causing those feelings. It is not, however, parroting or word-for-word repetition.

If your child comes in looking woebegone and says to you, "I'm not going to play with Casey and Jeff anymore because they won't share their dirt bikes with anyone," your normal response may be, "Well, why don't you find something else to do. They'll probably change their minds later." A better response would be one that does not console the child, but lets him know that you understand just how he feels—"You feel left out because they aren't sharing with you." This correctly describes the feelings behind your child's outward sadness; it lets him know that you are aware of those feelings. He may begin to pour out even more of his feelings at this point, possibly breaking down into sobs or tears. Allow it. Your child has found someone who understands, and he knows it. He feels free to express the hurt he presently feels. He knows he has found a friend he can trust. And trust is what we're building—an atmosphere of confidence that "my parents want what's best for me, and a brother or sister isn't going to change that fact."

Here are four secrets for being an active listener.

1. Give the child direct eye contact as he speaks, and think about the *person* behind the words. Many times when I'm cooking dinner

or folding laundry, our sons will come by and spin hair-raising tales of intrigue about invaders, wild Indians, or paramedics. Absorbed in my own thoughts, I find it easy just to drop an occasional "uh-huh" or "is that so?" I have discovered that our boys can come up with some very creative stuff. So I try to pay them more attention because listening allows me special access to a restricted area—their vibrant imaginations. I don't have to fix a penetrating gaze upon them every moment they're speaking. As I work, I occasionally glance up, smile and look right into those sparkling eyes. This is a considerable improvement over "uh-huh." Of course, there are also many times when I must give them my complete attention as I listen.

2. When trying to expose a child's feelings, don't ask questions that can be answered with only one word, such as "yes," "no," or "fine." Instead of, "Did you have fun in school today?" try "Tell me what happened at school."

3. Be very careful about putting words into his mouth. You will learn a lot more about your child if you will patiently wait for him to say what he really means. Have you ever felt the frustration of trying to explain a matter to someone, only to have that person continually second-guess you with questions which really weren't leading in the direction you wanted?

Consider this exchange that recently took place in our car on the way home from church.

Dad: Jonathan, what did you do in Sunday school today?
Jonathan: Well, we uh . . .
Christopher: Did you color?
Jonathan: Yes, but . . .
Christopher: Did you sing songs?
Jonathan: Yes, but . . .
Mom: Christopher, please be quiet for a minute.
Christopher: But I was going to ask him if Richie was there.
Jonathan: Yes, but . . .
Christopher: Was he sick?
Mom: Christopher, hush, please. Now, Jonathan, what were you trying to say?
Jonathan: I guess I forgot.

4. When your child confides in you, honor that confidence. If

your child unveils to you his personal problems, don't betray that trust by telling family members or friends. And don't seize the opportunity to jump on a soapbox and preach about the evils of what has been done. Help him arrive at his own conclusions by asking appropriate questions.

Suppose your daughter has gotten into trouble at school. Some parents would bring this up at the dinner table for everyone to discuss. Using this technique might damage your daughter's self-image, or her relationship with her siblings. (If they are aware of each other's every misdeed, they have powerful ammunition for future blackmail.)

The other side of the communication coin is, of course, what we parents say to our kids. We will discuss this in the next section. It's especially important to keep conversation on a positive note. Your child's image of himself will be largely composed of what we *say* he is.

Encouraging Words

When I was a child, one of my favorite stories was Mother's account of my birth. Because she is such a positive person, her telling of the story always made me feel that this event was one of the best things that ever happened to her and my father.

It's not surprising to us, therefore, that one of our sons' favorite narratives is our "family history," beginning with the year their daddy and I met at college and fell in love, moving through each much-wanted-and-loved baby, and up to the present threesome who have proven to be a greater delight than we ever imagined.

Each of us craves to know that we are important to someone. A child, especially, needs this, for he views the world through what seems to be a magnifying glass—everyone else seems bigger or more important than he is.

A child needs to be encouraged and uplifted almost constantly. His feelings of self-worth are quite fragile, and he depends on what he hears to help him understand who he is. He will usually live up to what is being said about him.

Several parents have mentioned the devastating effects that occurred when one child excelled in something and people said heartless things to the other, such as, "Wow! Your sister can really slug that ball! Are you as good as she is?" When a child sees his brother or sister receiving an abundance of commendations from outsiders (and sometimes even parents), he may seriously begin to wonder if the other child isn't a little more valuable. A pathway to resentment and hostility can be created almost without our being aware of it.

A child's self-esteem is a delicate part of his being. It can be crushed by an angry word, shattered by a disgusted look, and crumpled with a thoughtless deed. It can even be destroyed by seemingly much less—the apathetic absence of loving words and acts. Some kids appear to rebound quickly or to not need as much in the way of encouragement and praise, but this may be just the child's way of dealing with the shortage. A battered self-image still lies beneath the surface.

During the 13th century, Frederick II, Holy Roman emperor, conducted an unusual experiment among some children of his empire. Desiring to learn if children were born with a "natural" language, such as Greek, Latin, or Hebrew, he instructed the foster mothers and wet nurses to attend to the *physical* needs of their infant charges, but *never to speak to them*. They were also not allowed to play with the children or handle them excessively.

The monarch never learned what he set out to discover, however, because all the children *died* within a short time. Said a medieval writer, ". . . they could not live without the petting and joyful faces and loving words of their foster mothers."[13]

Praise reinforces desirable behavior. The Bible warns against "flattering lips" but exhorts us to go right ahead and "encourage each other and build each other up, just as in fact you are doing" (1 Thess. 5:11). In this passage, Paul not only tells his readers what to do, he shows them how it works by building them up at the same time (notice the last phrase).

In each of his epistles Paul offers abundant praise, always in a constructive manner: (1) He gave it directly to the people who deserved it (not "Why can't more of your churches be like the one in

Thessalonica?"); and (2) He didn't exaggerate or underrate anyone's efforts. He simply stated the facts.

Paul reinforced good behavior in an effort to develop *habits* among the early Christians. Praise is constructive when it is distributed in this way. It can become destructive if it is given in unbalanced proportions, or if it comes across as insincere flattery or something said just to "even the score." By spending time alone with each child you will discern his strengths and weaknesses. You will then have many opportunities to encourage him in his strong points and help him work on his weaknesses.

Children can learn to encourage and take pride in their siblings' accomplishments. This will be taught through a very gentle, gradual process, especially if there is an undercurrent of resentment that has not yet been resolved. The first step is helping each child discover just what his special gifts and abilities are. As he recognizes the fact that he also has talents to be developed, he can more easily accept the victories of others with grace.

One trick my mother used, which I have also found successful, is the knowing wink which elevates an older child to a position of near-adulthood, enabling him to share an "adult" secret about what might ordinarily seem unimportant. One day, when I was eight, my four-year-old sister was helping Mother in the kitchen. Before lunch Mom took me aside and, with a wink, said, "Susan's trying very hard to cut up the celery and pickles for our tuna salad. Maybe when we're eating you can help her feel good about it by telling her how yummy it is." Her wink informed me that I would be doing something grown-up if I didn't complain about the one-inch chunks of pickle in the salad.

I have used the same technique with our sons many times. A big brother has the potential of correcting almost everything a younger child says and does. But we explain to Chris thoroughly and often that a child three years younger can't be expected to know all that an older child has acquired. We enjoy watching Jonathan struggle to imitate something his brother is doing (e.g., tying shoes), and then looking over at Christopher and finding him winking and nodding at me saying, "You're really trying *hard,* Jonny!" Jonathan seems to appreciate more the encouragement he receives from his big brother than that which he gets from anyone else.

Anne Ortlund has provided an interesting viewpoint on this not-so-new idea of making positive, encouraging remarks that build others up. In her book, *Children Are Wet Cement,* she shows us how to affirm in our children the traits and fine details we hope to see. She writes:

> Tell God about your child—and second, *tell your child.* How he needs your support and affirmation! When he's new in this world, his security is a very tenuous thing. Every child needs heaps and gobs of affirmation. . . .
>
> The impressions words make, as they go into his ears and down into his heart and his concept of himself, are absolutely crucial. "As a (person) thinks in his heart, so is he."
>
> Over and over, put specific information into his storage box.
>
> I hadn't even clearly defined this technique when our first three were growing up, and yet I thank the Lord that He helped me to do it somewhat. Over and over, Ray and I told each child separately, "I can hardly wait till you grow up. You're going to stand out in a crowd! You're going to love the Lord; you're going to lead others in spiritual things; you're going to be a wonderful Christian adult. We'll be so proud of you."
>
> And it's true; each one has become that. We're telling our fourth child these things now.[14]

The day your child is born, begin giving affirmations—smiles and pleasant words designed to make a baby feel good about his new home and himself. You can say such things as, "We're so happy God sent you to us," or "You are making us so happy!" or "You will like living with us more each day," or "You are going to grow big and strong and do something special for God," or "You are very important to all of us."

Such words, spoken as you respond to him and interact, will begin the work of building up his concept of himself and giving him a sense of value before God. If you maintain these affirmations as your child grows, he too will acquire the habit of pointing out an appreciating goodness in others.

As your child grows older, tailor your affirmations to those areas in his life that are developing or that could stand improvement.

Anne Ortlund says it helps to give a child something to reach for, a personal ideal.

You might say to a five-year-old, "You are becoming more and more responsible," or "You are doing things so carefully these days," or "You are teaching your little sister so many new things!"

You might say to a ten-year-old, "You are becoming better and better about doing your homework without being reminded," or "You are becoming very considerate of others."

To a teenager you might say, "I can envision you as an outstanding college student," or "It's so exciting to see God make you into a man (or woman) able to serve Him!"

Once you acquire the habit, you will find it easy to see the possibilities for affirming your children's attitudes toward one another and the family in general. Even the tiniest children can benefit from positive, encouraging statements. The power of suggestion is much stronger than most people realize. Your children will actually become much of what you tell them they are, and that includes becoming loving siblings. Affirmations such as the following may be very helpful for this: "You are a kind person." "You like to make people happy." "You like to help people. You help Daddy. You help Mommy. You help big sister, Mary, too." "You are careful with babies. I know you will be a kind big brother." "Our whole family is happy that God gave us Jennifer."

Most of us don't need to be reminded of the results of negative "affirmations." It seems that any time we caution our kids *not* to do something, they derive great pleasure from trying it. When Jonathan was not even two, I remember seeing him stalking around the house caveman-style with a plastic baseball bat in tow. Since I was headed out to the garage to start a load of laundry, I issued a thoughtless warning before leaving: "Jonathan, if you're going to carry that bat, be careful that you don't hit any people with it" (there was only one person in question—his big brother). Not two seconds later I heard a loud whack, then a yowl that could have been mistaken for an air-raid warning. I turned to see Jonathan making his getaway, bat still clutched in his chubby fist. He had never before hit anyone with anything. I think he found my suggestion to be so intriguing that he had to try it out. Shame on me!

Parent Talk

1. Think of a parent (or a couple) who communicates well with his children. Later on, spend an hour "role-playing," trying to respond to your children as you think that parent would. Notice how your children respond to you. If your responses are successful, try for another hour.
2. For each child you have, list 10 fitting affirmations. Make a point during the next week to build up each child's sense of worth at every opportunity.

Family Time

1. Have each child take a turn describing himself, naming at least three qualities which make him unique.
2. Have each family member name at least one positive quality possessed by each of the other members.

8

Spiritual Guidance:
Reinforcing the Roots

> These commandments that I give you today are to be upon your hearts. Impress them on your children. Talk about them when you sit at home and when you walk along the road, when you lie down and when you get up. Tie them as symbols on your hands and bind them on your foreheads. Write them on the doorframes of your house and on your gates. If you pay attention to these laws and are careful to follow them, then the Lord your God will keep his covenant of love with you (Deut. 6:6-9; 7:12).

When Christopher was just a few days old, I can remember his daddy often holding him in one sturdy hand and clasping his Bible in the other. "Son," he would say, "if you never learn anything else, remember this: The Bible is the Word of God, and Jesus is the Son of God. Don't ever forget that."

During some of the long nights that followed, when our son thought daytime was for sleeping and nighttime for eating, I would cradle him in my arms in the big rocking chair and sing every gospel song, old hymn, every little chorus I could recall, hoping to convey to him that we and God loved him—even if he didn't have any respect for our sleeping hours. In the daytime, I read to him from the

Bible during my personal devotions—if he happened to be awake.

A few months later, after we had finished college and gotten settled in our new home, we began having family devotions. I can still picture our roly-poly six-month-old collapsing into fits of toothless giggles as his daddy performed all kinds of voice inflections, gestures, and gyrations trying to make it interesting for him. He succeeded.

Our kids need to understand and desire to do what God expects of them. This is crucial if we want them to "walk in love." While we as adults conduct ourselves on the basis of many years' growth, training, and experience (and we're still not perfect), we sometimes forget that our children are not born knowing how to always do the right thing. That's one of the reasons they have parents—to gently nurture them toward acceptable behavior. This training can be more easily accomplished by parents who foster a love for and knowledge of the Word of God. Only when a child is familiar with what the Bible says can he proceed to the next step—obeying its instructions and making them part of his life. In *How to Raise Your Children for Christ*, Andrew Murray says:

> Scripture needs the believing parent as its messenger. The believing parent needs scripture as the vehicle for the communication of his faith. . . . One of the highest honors God has for the believing parent is that He has made him the minister of His holy Word to his children.[15]

Bringing the Word to our children is something that must be planned. It will not be effective if presented as a preachy, after-the-fact reprimand ("Why did you hit her? Don't you know the Bible tells us to be kind to one another?"). Parents often take the task of conviction into their own hands instead of leaving it to the Holy Spirit, who does it most tactfully and effectively. He can do a fine job when the Word of God is being instilled regularly in the child.

Have you ever pondered a tough decision when suddenly, almost surprisingly, a very appropriate verse from Scripture just "popped" into your mind and gave the answer? The more familiar a person is with the Word of God, the more frequently this happens. Those answers, instructions and guidelines, are usually words we have retained at another time, and are brought back to us by the Holy Spirit at the moment we need them.

Of course this can work for children too. Our role as parents is to bring the Word of God to each child, making sure it gets filed away in his amazing, sponge-like memory banks. Then the Holy Spirit takes over in the critical moments, reminding a tormented brother or sister to "be kind to one another" or "overcome evil with good." This isn't "programming," in a mechanistic sense, however, for he must choose to obey or disobey God's command.

It usually takes quite a bit of trial, error, and experience for a person to learn that it's a good idea to respond to the nudgings of the Holy Spirit. Just like we do, kids will make many mistakes. But I firmly believe that the earlier they are exposed to the Christian life and the adventure of the Christian walk, the more it will help them, and the better off they'll be. If your children are still quite young, be thankful. Your efforts in this area have endless possibilities.

Scripture memorization is probably the most obvious method. Once these words are "hidden in the heart" the Holy Spirit will cause them to be recalled at times when they are needed most. (Verses pertaining to relationships with people can be very significant in sibling crises.) Even young children who can barely talk can lisp a short verse of three or four words; this makes them feel important because they are participating in the same activity they see the rest of the family doing.

We often employ incentives to encourage our sons to memorize. Our two oldest sons' birthdays are both in the winter, as is Christmas, and their bikes seem to always fall apart in the summer. Obviously we can't make them wait six months for a new set of wheels, so we have had both our boys "earn" their latest vehicles. For instance, we told Christopher that when he learned one new verse for each letter of the alphabet he could have a new bike. That boy worked! In only three weeks he had learned his quota—and he has retained them by frequent review. Jonathan was just two and a half when his hand-me-down trike collapsed. Yet, he was able to learn six short verses in three weeks.

Review of your child's storehouse of Bible pearls provides a good activity when you are cooking or driving along in the car. One way is to begin reciting a passage, pausing at a significant word and allowing your child to "fill in the blanks." For Christopher we might try, "Love thy _____ as thy_____." For Jonathan the verses are simpler: "God is _____." At the back of this book you will find lists of suggested verses that you can help your children learn. All are geared toward helping your child learn to love and respond to God, and to love others—including his brothers and sisters.

One creative mother I know has had great fun and success with fitting Bible verses with tunes and teaching her children to sing their verses. Remember our Marine friend at boot camp that I mentioned earlier? He told us that as they marched along they'd sing a string of little ditties that reminded them of what their purpose was, and of the fact that they were Marines—the best. Words put to rhythm and music are much easier to recall than words alone. Besides that, it's very hard to sing a lilting melody and have a grumpy frown on one's face at the same time. Singing has a marvelous power to brighten the atmosphere of a home.

Christian songs are another tool for instilling good thought patterns. Think back to some of the songs you sang as a child in Sunday school or at camp. If they're memorable to you, chances are that your children will enjoy them too. You can't remember all the words? Make up some new ones. Or invent lyrics that are more appropriate for what you are trying to teach. We have taught our children the old standard, "The B-I-B-L-E." But the original words say, "I stand alone on the Word of God." I have never met a child yet who knew what it means to "stand" on the Word of God (except in the literal sense), and it's a very difficult metaphor to explain to a one-, or two-, or even seven-year-old. We have changed that particular line to, "I love to learn from the Word of God." Again, it helps accomplish our purpose of "teaching" them to enjoy and respond to God's Word and will.

Older children, grades four through the teen years, are not only exceptional memorizers, but they love games. Channel their competitive urges and play scripture games with them. One that anyone who reads can play is a Bible Treasure Hunt, where a point is given to the first person who can find a verse in a certain chapter with, for example, the word "love." Or a verse in Romans 12 about "affection." Or have them look for a verse in 1 Thessalonians 4 that contains the word "brotherly." This game will take a little advance preparation in order to locate verses that will be most meaningful to the children's development. Of course there's always the good old-fashioned Sword Drill, where the leader gives a reference and the contestants scramble to see who can locate it first in their Bibles. Kids never seem to tire of this one, and with a good concordance or topical Bible, one hardly even has to plan ahead.

The key to keeping your children's interest level high will probably lie in some sort of external motivation or reward. Some people think of this as bribery and refuse to stoop so low, but it's really no more of a bribe for you to offer your child points, stars, snacks or toys, than it is for your employer to offer you a paycheck for a week's work. We all need incentives. Children respond better to tangible things. A few pieces of sugarless gum or a chart with stickers to help them see how important we feel the Word of God is are a small price to pay.

Your family will gain much enjoyment and build many happy memories if you establish some sort of regular "family time" to impart your values and goals to the children. This could be a lengthened version of family devotions, perhaps held once a week. If the children are young, you will have to plan and carry out most of what is done, but as your children reach school age, they can create presentations of their own. Teens will often amaze their families with the extent of their creative abilities in this area.

Since our sons are still quite young, we handle family night in this manner: We begin by together singing a few of the children's favorite songs, and usually one hymn. Then we go through our traditional recitation of: "The Bible is the Word of God and Jesus is the Son of God." After this, Ralph reads two stories from children's Bible story books—one geared to Christopher's level and one that Jonathan can understand. He then asks questions about the story events to find out if the boys have comprehended. Then we either read other books aloud for a while, or we play a board game, or do something equally fun. Sometimes I make popcorn to add to the festivities. Family night is a good time to play the aforementioned Bible games and to pull everyone together in dialogue.

Daily family devotions can become tedious if they are lengthy and boring. You must constantly search for fresh ideas and new approaches in order to keep the practice lively and fun. There are many excellent devotional books available, geared to the needs of various ages. One of my favorite for families with young children is *Today I Feel Like a Warm Fuzzy* by William Coleman. Others are listed at the back of this book. The best time for family devotions seems to be in the evening, when people are in less of a hurry. Right after supper is a good time, or, if your children still act civilized just before bedtime, that can be a good time slot. Just before supper is the worst time, because most are preoccupied with hunger pangs, and the domestic manager (Mom) is probably having a hard enough time keeping everything synchronized.

Daily devotions should be short (you'd be surprised at what will fit into 5-8 minutes), interesting to the age level of the children involved, and practical. Use this as a time of ministering to your children's needs, fears, misconceptions, and weaknesses. Try not to be preachy or condemning. Keep the message low-key and let the Holy Spirit do the work.

In addition to family devotions, a child who is old enough to know Christ and to read can be encouraged to begin his own personal devotional time. One couple rewarded their son's graduation from kindergarten by buying him a nightstand and a lamp and extending his bedtime by one-half hour, with the stipulation that the time be used for reading in bed.

Besides this structured approach, there are many teaching moments in every day, times in which you can gently and non-threateningly remind a child of what God says about this or that. Jonathan and I watched one morning as some panic-stricken seagulls winged rapidly overhead, trying to escape an ominously black storm that was rolling in.

He then said, "Why does God call them *sea*gulls?" Readily, I took the opportunity to explain that they were birds that liked to live near the sea, but that the dark storm clouds were making them want to leave for a while.

"Are they scared?"

"It looks like they may be. But the Bible tells us that God is watching them right now and He will take care of them, just like He takes care of us. Each of us is very special to Him, you know."

Incidents occur every day which can be related to a biblical teaching. We can exploit these opportunities just as Jesus used illustrations from the world around Him to clarify things for His followers. As our children receive these truths in a relevant context, the Bible will become real to them and they will be inspired to follow God's direction in their own lives.

As you expose your children to the riches of God's Word, you will also be introducing them to the friend who is closer than a brother, Jesus Christ. There is nothing so sweet as a young child who is so familiar with the name of Jesus that he speaks of Him like one would a relative or close family friend. Children who are brought up in a Christian home, led by parents who are walking, breathing examples of the Spirit-filled life, often come to a personal faith in Christ as Savior at a remarkably early age. Once such a conversion has transpired, parents will find their child's spiritual growth and development a fascinating process.

Talk to your kids about Jesus, just as you talk about Grandma and Grandpa or other family friends. They have great faith. As a "mature" adult, I have never quite been able to imagine how I will react when I meet Jesus face-to-face, but children don't have that problem. One of ours said, "When Jesus comes back I'm going to show Him that I can load my own toothbrush now!"

We have five chairs at our dinner table. One night, as we were eating, Christopher asked me who the fifth chair was for (this was before the birth of our third son). Although it was really just an extra, I said, "Well, we could use that chair to remind us that Jesus is right here with us as we eat." I wasn't sure this was a good idea, knowing the way kids twist things around at times, but it was too late, I had already spoken. The boys, however, liked that idea, and have, since then, often reminded a guest that he is fortunate enough to be sitting in "God's chair." As we affirm that our Lord is a special companion, an honored guest, one who truly is with us at all times, a child will *want* to please Him—because he knows God cares.

The Spirit-filled Christian life provides an abundance of spiritual riches. But all the precious truths God is showing us deserves to be passed along. Children are never too young to appreciate God's goodness and to learn obedience to God.

Parent Talk

1. Discuss: Have we been faithful to plant the Word of God in our children's lives? How could we improve in this endeavor?
2. Plan together your next family devotional time. Discuss: How can we make it interesting and applicable to our children? What resources shall we use? What song(s) shall we sing? What is the best time of day for this? Then *do* it!

Family Time

If your children are accustomed to regular family devotions, give them a chance to lead once in a while. Assign each child a brother or sister partner and give them a week or so to prepare a program. They can tell a story, perform a skit, use puppets, lead a discussion, or whatever else their imaginations will allow.

9

Postive Programming:
The Perfect Plant Food

When our first child was about two-and-a-half, Jackie, a former
Lamaze student of mine, came over with her new baby and her boy
who was about four. As we conversed in the living room, the boys
played outside on the patio, and my guest kept glancing out the
screen door in the direction of the children. I couldn't figure out what
they were doing that she found so intriguing—and far be it from me
to interfere when two kids are playing quietly (for a change).

I was about to ask her what was the matter when she stepped to
the door and called to them. "Boys . . ."

It was so sudden that it took me by surprise; I hadn't seen them
doing anything mischievous.

But instead of reprimanding them, she continued, "We sure
appreciate that you guys are playing together so nicely. It really
makes us happy. Thank you for sharing your toys."

I'm sure I did not conceal my amazement. We had been very diligent to praising our son when he did all those remarkable things a
first child does, but it had never once occurred to us to tell him how

happy it made us when he simply treated another person with kindness.

Jackie returned to her place on the couch and picked up the conversation like she did her knitting—almost without thinking. It seemed so effortless for her to speak to her child in that way. She was practicing a form of prevention we might call "positive programming."

Dr. Dobson alludes to this in his book, *Hide or Seek*: "Adults should devote their creative energies to the teaching of love and dignity. . . . Children are destructive to the weak and lowly because we adults haven't bothered to *teach* them to 'feel' for one another."[16]

Anything we parents can do—consciously—to enhance the relationships between our children falls into the category of programming. Remember the concept of fire prevention? Most of the time it never occurs to us that there are certain measures we can take to defuse a potentially explosive condition before it has a chance to ignite. A large part of this defusing will be verbal in nature. Consider an example.

Two of your children are wrapped up in the same blanket on your couch, looking at a book. Many mothers, including myself, would tend to just keep quiet, thinking that to say anything would somehow break the "spell." But it is an excellent opportunity to stop and say something positive, such as, "You two look as snug as a couple of bugs. I'll bet you're glad that you have each other to spend time with?" This remark will go much further than saying, the next time they're arguing, "Will you two cut it out? You should be *grateful* you have each other. Some kids wish for a brother or sister and never get one!"

Keep an eye open for instances that merit special attention: "That was nice of Billy to give you the rest of his dessert," or "You girls look so sweet when you're playing house like that," or "Remember how lonely it used to be before we had Jennifer?" or "Isn't it nice that Mike got a vacation from school so he could spend the day with us?"

Parents can also purposely mention things to each other when the little ones are within earshot (and they always seem to be listening!). "You should have seen your sons in the mud today. They were having a great time playing together." Or "You'll never guess what Jan did for Richie today. She spent about an hour pulling him up and down the sidewalk in his wagon. She's such a good big sister for him."

The supper table provides a good time for such programming. It is a time when everyone is winding down, and when some family members need to be informed of the day's activities. We have two rules for our dinner hour: Only one person talks at a time, and no bad reports are allowed. We deal with problems and disciplinary matters in private, later on.

We have always tried to stress to our youngsters the concept that we are a team. We have never wanted our children to feel that we are five individuals who happen to live in the same house. We want them to know that there is something very special about our relationship and that we are all irreplaceable members of a unit that functions together.

Ralph is especially good at turning routine projects into *team* efforts. One day the boys were playing ball in the backyard when their softball landed on the patio roof and stayed there. Ralph could have easily lifted one boy up on the roof or gotten the ball down himself, but instead he made it a cooperative effort. He had Jonathan climb into the treehouse and act as "spotter" while he hoisted Christopher up and had him move the ball with a stick according to Jonny's directions. Jonathan dashed in moments later to tell me how they had "croperated" to retrieve the ball. He was proud to be a part of the team.

We also attempt to have every member of our family know where every other member is all the time. When it is impossible for us all to be together, we talk about the "missing member," what he is probably doing at the moment, and when we expect to see him again. When one of us goes someplace, we often take one or both boys with us. We work together around the house and in the yard. We sit together in church. We eat as a family. We need each other, and we want our sons to recognize the sense of unity that comes from being an important part of "the team."

Verbal Programming

Many parents have created innovative, positive programming ideas. They constantly look for the right moments to help their children appreciate each other. One mother makes up little stories with fictionalized characters that help her children think through ways of dealing with each other.

Another mother said, "As a child, my favorite thing to play with my mother was, 'What would you do if . . .' We have adapted this to help our children premeditate actions and reactions." During private moments she asks a child questions such as, "What would you do if you found that Kimmy had gotten out your new race car set and broken one of the cars?" or "What would you do if Bobby were invited to a birthday party and you weren't?" or "What would you do if you wanted to play catch with Steve and he wasn't in the mood?" or "What would you do if the teachers at school kept calling you 'Linda Green's little brother'?"

Such conversations provide the child a chance to rehearse possible solutions to a problem while he is calm and collected, and without fear of reprimand for doing the wrong thing. He can bounce his ideas off someone he trusts, and may think about these things long after the conversation has ended. This is why Bruce Narramore writes, "The time for instruction is generally before or after a conflict, when emotions are at a reasonable level."[17]

Special Activities

A project I have enjoyed in my mothering years is making picture books for our sons, using family photographs to illustrate the text. First I leaf through our albums and boxes of not-yet-mounted pictures, finding one suitable for whatever theme I have chosen. Then I work on the text—nothing fancy or poetic, just simple language saying what I want it to say. I paste the pictures on sheets of construction paper, write the text with a felt maker, cover each page with clear contact paper, then fasten the pages together with yarn, brads, rings, or ribbon.

My first effort was a book for Christopher entitled "My Daddy." Chris was two at the time. It emphasized all the things his dad was capable of doing and how much fun they had together. Ralph has enjoyed that book every bit as much as the boys have. Later, when Jonathan turned one, I made one for him about all the people who loved him. There also is one in the works about grandparents. The most popular, however, has been our family book entitled "Brothers." Although the pictures add to the personality of the book, I will include only the text:

> On November 26, 1978, when Jonathan joined the Milburn family, we became BROTHERS.
> Not everyone is lucky enough to have a brother, but we both are.
> An older brother is handy to have. He can show me how to do things.
> He lets me borrow his toys!
> He can help me take a bath.
> And he's cozy to sleep beside!
> He's a leader I can depend on.
> A younger brother is special too. He's a friend to play with.
> When he follows me around it makes me feel VERY important!
> And he makes my bathtime almost FUN!
> He keeps me company at nap time. Life's a lot more exciting than it used to be!
> Brothers share the same mommy,
> The same daddy,
> And the same grandparents.
> They also share a lot of laughs —
> And a lot of love!
> The Bible reminds me to LOVE my brother.
> With a brother like mine,
> THAT'S EASY!

Each line above represents a different page and a different photo. I made certain that I devoted the same number of pages to each child so there would never be any argument over who got the most lines. We had fun working together on this project. And the boys like our homemade books best because they are so personal.

An inexpensive camera will not only help you with a project such as this one, but if you make a habit of photographing your children when they are doing things together, your pictures will be a source of delight later on. Our children love to get out the picture albums and look at themselves as they were a few years earlier. We use this as part of our "programming" too: "Aw, look, there you both are, asleep on the floor," or "Isn't that nice how you guys helped Dad in the yard?" or "You fellows make a great baseball team!"

Teach Them to Laugh!

Laughter reduces friction. We can help our children cultivate the ability to laugh problems off—to take a little more from others. Parents who are very serious about life often raise children who are equally solemn. There's nothing wrong with being a serious person, but there is much to be gained by learning to not let little things bother us. Our own reactions usually determine how our children will react to things.

One Saturday evening we were holding a big family dinner at my parents' home. After the meal I decided to take my nephew Jimmy across the street to visit a neighbor. We crossed the family's sloping front yard in the dark and climbed some flagstone steps to reach the porch. As my friends and I were conversing at the front door, we heard a shuffling sound in the darkness and several thumps. Eighteen-month-old Jimmy had lost his footing and tumbled down about three steps. He was sitting on the ground, with lower lip protruding and chin quivering, looking as if he was deciding whether or not to cry.

Almost before he'd even landed, though, this lady, a teacher, began applauding and saying to him, "Well, aren't you a clever little boy, to roll down like that and land sitting up! I'll bet that was *fun*, wasn't it? Tell me, how did you do that?" My nephew's upside-down mouth crinkled into a proud smile, and he stood up without a whimper. That neighbor's quick action had tempered his reaction—he was learning to laugh about minor misfortune.

Another day I saw one of our sons walk past his brother (who was sprawled across the floor playing with cars) and accidentally stumble over his legs. He landed, as you might guess, flat on his face, and his dour countenance told me he was on the verge of blowing up at his brother for causing him such humiliation. I realized a little humor would lighten up the situation, so instead of saying something dull and predictable such as, "Oh, dear, are you all right?" I tried, "Well! Did you have a nice *trip?*" He found my remark sufficiently funny, soon forgot his mishap, and began playing with his brother.

Some folks are natural "gloomers," spreading depression and frustration to anyone who will listen. Others are "bloomers," who add a spring-fresh brightness to the lives of those they know. I still have fond memories of my first year in college; my three roommates and I spent almost the entire year laughing. Our shared good times developed a love for one another that continues to this day. It also enabled us to live with (and even joke about) those minor irritations that are bound to creep in when four people share close quarters.

What is the laughter level of your home? Do you enjoy lots of chuckles and giggles and good, old-fashioned belly laughs? Children can learn to project cheerful, happy, pleasant personalities. In fact, this is one of the easier lessons to teach because a smile brings its own reward—it makes others happy and makes the smiler feel better. "A cheerful heart is good medicine, but a crushed spirit dries up the bones" (Prov. 17:22).

By providing this "medicine" for each other, brothers and sisters will discover that their siblings are not just "tolerable," but actually a lot of fun.

Giving

One day shortly before Christmas, our boys were poring over a catalog, oohing and ahhing at all the remarkable toys. Every sentence for about five minutes began with, "I want . . ."

Feeling that this was not the healthiest of situations, I tried to channel their enthusiasm by saying, "You know, so close to Christmas, we should be thinking hard about what we're going to do for *other* people. It's always so much fun to see how happy they are when they open the gifts we have given. Why don't you see if you can think of something nice to give your cousins, Jimmy and Jenni. And, of course, you'll want to give things to each other, too."

"Here, let me help you . . ." one son piped to the other. My heart leaped—then plummeted as he continued, ". . . decide what you're getting *me*!"

God's love overflows with the attitude of giving. Therefore, the ability to cheerfully give (and give *in*) will be a very important trait for our children to acquire. Like so many other fine character qualities, children rarely acquire this one on their own. They learn it form the example we set and our accompanying attitude.

Generosity is most effective when spread into every corner of our lives. It does little good to nag our children about sharing if we turn around and say, "I'm not wasting *my* day chauffeuring Mrs. Smith to the doctor. If she wants a ride she can call a cab."

Charity begins at home, but if charity also ends there, its life will be brief. We must help our children find the joy experienced in giving even when there is sacrifice. As they discover this, they will have a greater willingness to give to those who live with them under the same roof.

How many times have we heard a pastor, missionary or close friend say to you, "Keep us in your prayers"? We always nod and smile and say, "Of course"—but it's hard to fulfill a promise on a systematic basis. Having attended Bible college for four years, we have an abundance of friends who are in the pastorate, on the mission field, or in other full-time Christian work. We have kept in touch with many through the years, and attempt to do our part by upholding them in prayer.

We eventually have found an easy and fun way that not only accomplishes this purpose, but involves our children and helps them capture the spirit of giving. We have obtained photographs of most of the families, or at least the children in those families, from correspondence, Christmas cards, yearbook photos, vacation pictures, or prayer cards. We paste each onto a 3 × 5 card that also contains the family's name, their location, and any special need they might have. We also have cards for our pastor and church staff, close family friends, and various relatives. Every evening at dinner we take out one card and talk about the people on it. The boys are always fascinated to see pictures of children their age who live in "exotic" places such as Mexico, Korea or New York. We tell our sons what kind of ministry the family is involved in or why they need our prayers; we then pray for them as we say our table grace. We find it rewarding to sense our sons' genuine compassion as they pray for Grampy's cough, or for a pastor's son they have never met who has a learning disability, or for the family of six with newborn twins.

Another opportunity for teaching generosity is the use of cast-offs. Of course, some things become so worn that it would be offensive to offer them to someone else, but many times we dispose of good clothes, toys, and household items because they no longer have value to us. When Christopher outgrows an item of clothing, I seize the opportunity to make it a learning experience. I may say, "Well, look at that! You must have grown two inches overnight. Those pants come all the way up to your ankles! We'll have to get you a new pair soon. Tell you what, to make room for some new ones in your drawer, why don't we pass those along to Jonny?" Then, usually very ceremoniously, he will present them to his younger brother, who always seems delighted to have acquired something that was worn by his hero.

Before the recent birth of our third son, when Jonathan outgrew something, we would go through the same process, but I would say, "Let's see, whom do we know that might fit this shirt?" Handily, he has a boy cousin slightly smaller than he, so usually we have no problem in finding a joyful recipient.

With toys we do the same thing. Before last Christmas we told them that this year there wouldn't be room for new toys—unless we *made* room by giving some beforehand to unfortunte children. Together we sorted through everything and decided which toys would be donated to a charity and which were too badly damaged to be given to anyone. They also selected, from the "charity" assortment, a few nice things, which they wrapped themselves and gave to their little cousins as Christmas presents. This requires more sacrifice than if they had gone into a store with us and "picked" something which was then paid for by Mom and Dad. And they were very interested in watching Jimmy and Jenni open *their* gifts.

You must build and encourage at times when your children are not at each other's throats. If one has a possession that is deeply coveted by another, sometimes when neither is using it suggest, privately, "Becky, remember how much Julie likes your play jewelry? Wouldn't she be surprised if you offered to let her play with it right now while you're coloring?"

There are other ways to emphasize the blessings of giving. If your children earn or receive some money, talk with them about tithing and the fun of dropping money in the offering bank at Sunday school. When the offering is taken in the worship service, make sure they have something to put in, even if it's just a few jingly coins. (And remember, they'll be watching to see what *you* give!) Notice the glee on the face of a child who has just deposited a fistful of nickels into the Salvation Army pot. If you have a gift for someone, let your child present it, coaching him beforehand with something like, "Mrs. Painter has really helped me by playing the piano in my Sunday school class. I thought we could give her this writing paper as a thank you. Would you like to take it to her?" I did this with Jonathan and Mrs. Painter even got a spontaneous kiss in the bargain!

Courtesy

Hand-in-hand with teaching generosity should be teaching courtesy and respect. If you have ever observed a playground full of children, you realize the immensity of such a task. But I believe that often the lack of these qualities occurs because instruction has been *overlooked*. Basically, instruction is a matter of setting the right examples and helping them develop pleasant habits.

As a parent, I am very familiar with the temptation to save the "polite" words for outsiders. After all, when we want something done, we want it done *now*, and to tack on a "will you please" adds at least another half-second to the process. Some parents (fathers are more guilty of this, I think) even feel that their authority is undermined if they do not bark out orders like an Army sergeant. Children, however, respond better and faster to those who treat them with courtesy. If we habitually use pleasantries such as, "Excuse me, please," "Oh, I'm sorry," "Thank you," and "You're welcome," our children will acquire them as habits, just as they acquire the rest of our language.

I was shocked when Ralph and I were first married and he thanked me for cooking a meal. But he has done it consistently since then and I am no longer shocked by it—just flattered. Perhaps not too surprisingly, our sons also thank me for each meal, without prompting. I know why they have learned the habit.

Mike Phillips suggests in his book, *Building Respect, Responsibility, and Spiritual Values in Your Child,* that a small reward be given every time courtesy is practiced—until it becomes a thoroughly ingrained habit. Mike and his wife, Judy, told me personally that they consider the use of courtesy words to be a major contributing factor in helping their children get along together. They are convinced that what may begin as "mere words" will become an attitude if practiced long enough. Speaking calmly and respectfully to others is probably the very essence of the "soft answer" that "turneth away wrath" (Prov. 15:1, KJV).

Also in the realm of courtesy is the need to teach children acceptable ways to *disagree*. Most significant will be the example they see in you. If you handle well your own confrontations, there will be fewer problems than one might expect. However, if you have fallen into patterns of yelling, griping, and bossing, it will take some practice to correct the situation.

Role-playing sessions can be a fun way to learn good habits for disagreement. Present your children with some appropriate "what ifs." After they have given their responses, guide them to find ways of improving wording or tone of voice in order to reflect love and respect. Teach them to say things like, "Thanks for letting me skate with you, but I think I'd like to quit now," or "David, please put my calculator back where you found it," or "Excuse me, Karen, but you're in the way," or "I really don't want to do it that way, but I'll try your idea if you'll try mine."

Besides helping your children with their spoken exchanges, you can be on the lookout for instances when your children can *do* things to help one another. Make suggestions when you feel they might be well-received. A bond develops between two people who have helped each other out. Our boys think it's fun to run and get each other's shoes or to help one another fasten belts and buttons. Christopher can usually be depended on to buckle up his brother's seat belt, and Jonathan will leap at the chance to bring his brother's bike into the garage. We encourage this whenever they seem "willing." (Of course, nobody would want to do this all the time—that would spoil the fun of it!) We try to recognize acts of kindness and laud them.

We easily fall into the habit of speaking up only when we are bothered or unhappy with something. This is why, for an occasional family night, it would be worthwhile to have a "speak out session," with the twist being, "Tonight we are going to talk about what we *like* about each other."

Parent Talk

1. Make a list of occasions in the past week in which you could have reinforced pleasant behavior in your children. Did you do it?
2. Resolve that beginning today, you will look for moments when your children are being kind to each other and tell them how much you appreciate it.

Family Time

1. Conduct a role-playing session, in which you describe a hypothetical situation to your children and let them act out their responses to one another. Example: "Janie, if you are trying to sweep the floor and Bobby's feet are in the way, what would you do?" Or, "Sheryl, you think Traci has taken a book from your room without permission, but you're not sure. What might you say to her?"
2. Brainstorm courtesy phrases such as, "Excuse me," "Please," and "Thank you." Make your list as long as possible.
3. Next time there's a lot of in-house clutter to pick up, organize a contest between your kids: offer a prize for the child who can pick up and put away the most items *belonging to someone else.*

10

Limits: Fencing Out the Invaders

Susan wants to spend the night with Shari, who doesn't meet with Susan's parents' approval. After the initial "no," Susan pleads and begs. Still a "no." She bargains and cajoles. Mom covers her ears and tries her best to ignore the pitiful antics. Susan hounds and harasses some more. Mom leaves the room. In desperation, Susan cries out, "You *never* let me do anything fun. You don't even love me!" Mother throws up her hands and says, "Oh, go ahead. Go *anywhere*. Stay all week if you like. I don't care *what* you do." Whereupon Susan's mouth drops open and emits a bewildered, "Huh?" Sound familiar?

Kids are funny. They'll con, wheedle, whine, beg, bribe, and blackmail a parent to let them do some forbidden thing; but if the parent actually gives in ("Just this once, mind you!"), they react with almost incredulous disappointment. Children often test the boundaries just to find out how secure they are. They really do want limits, and they need them. Children expect reasonable limits to be enforced consistently.

I'm not suggesting we routinely squelch all our kids' plans for good times, but rather that we set boundaries when they seem needed, then enforce them until the children are able to make wise decisions on their own.

I was impressed by the number of parents who have expressed to me the necessity of enforcing limits on what their children could do to each other. One mother said, "When I was little, I felt my parents wouldn't stop me from doing or saying *anything* to my sister. They might frown, or say, 'Now, that's not nice,' but they never really *made* me stop being cruel. It was as if they didn't think it was right to interfere."

Many parents today are under the impression that they should not become involved in their children's disputes and should let them work out these problems themselves. Even some Christian counselors advocate this. One writes, "The best way to solve sibling conflicts is to let the children battle it out for themselves. . . . Our children rarely want to hurt each other."[18] I disagree.

Scripture and secular history show us many children who did try to hurt one another. Esau vowed, saying, "The day of mourning for my father are near; then I will *kill* my brother Jacob" (Gen. 27:41). Charles Swindoll, after reading to his congregation the entire account of Jacob's chicanery, said:

> "A sensitive parent will detect such thoughts. A child that carries hatred in his heart cannot hide it for long—and won't hide it. It may come out in stoic silence; it may come to the surface in angry gestures. But the parent who sees it cannot afford to be passive. You let it go by; you think it will work itself out; you live with this kind of grudge between your children; and you'll see the day when, if he doesn't take his life, he'll treat him as though he were dead. It's incredible what the human heart will do when pressed to the extreme.
>
> "I'll confess . . . this has not been one of the bigger plagues we've had to wrestle with, because we've *dealt* with it. We've been on it like a hen on a junebug—every time it happens we get right down on it."[19]

James Dobson stresses that parents should not be afraid to become judge and legislator for their children. He reminds us that "in a community of no law and order there is more likelihood of living in hostility and conflict than of living in peace."[20]

One parent said, "We have specific punishments for specific actions. [The children] are not allowed to call names or hurt one another without paying the penalty—and we try to always make our punishments more trouble than they're worth." While it seems like a time-consuming task, many parents have established peace in their households by upholding the law and saying, "This (whatever it is) will no longer be tolerated. If it happens, the consequences will be. . . ."

This might be initiated with more success if you can sit down with your children and talk the matter over. You might say, "Julie and Jack, we have been noticing for some time now that there's a lot of name-calling going on between you two. We're not happy about it. You are too special to each other to be hurting one another's feelings with such nastiness. Let's read Proverbs 10 (or just certain verses of that chapter) together, then Proverbs 21:23." Discuss the various aspects of the problem, then ask them if they have a suggestion for a solution.

With teens or grade-school-age children, you might try making them pay (you) in real money or chores for any infringements. Make sure the price is high enough to hurt. Smaller children seem to respond best to isolation, either in their own room, Mom's room, the bathroom, or just standing in a corner for a few minutes. Being the social creatures that most of them are, corner-standing usually is payment enough.

Children can treat one another quite graciously if it just isn't profitable to be mean. If the usual sanctions do not seem to work, suspect that there is a problem other than just sibling rivalry; there is probably a lack of respect for your authority, and this needs to be dealt with. Many excellent books on child rearing discuss this issue far more thoroughly and accurately than I could, so consult them. The important thing is to take the leadership that your child is questioning, and show him that you are, without a doubt, in control.

It is entirely possible that what you see as sibling rivalry is not really rivalry at all, in that it is not rooted in jealousy, hatred, resentment, or unmet needs. Your children may simply be experiencing the effects of what I call "externals"—factors that, from the outside, erode that which you have so carefully nurtured. Three of these come to mind instantly.

Peers

A child needs friends. Every child should build a variety of friendships outside the home. In this way he learns how others live; he can acquire new interests and skills he might not be exposed to by you; he can learn ways of dealing with others diplomatically. Such ideals for your children's friendships cannot be allowed to develop haphazardly.

A child will pick up not only the "good" from these kids, but any bad examples they have to offer as well. Every family has different standards for the behavior of its young people, and you will find many parents who do not have the same level of concern for their kids' development as you do for yours. If a sibling pair your children see a lot seem to have an intense hatred for each other, this will not go unabsorbed by your children. In most cases, the pressure to please peers and to be like them is too strong for a child to withstand alone. When a child is young, he copies others just for the sake of copying. As he grows older, he thinks it is necessary to imitate whoever is "on top" in order to survive socially.

A Christian school principal we know believes that peers are the "single most powerful influence on children of all ages." Another educational expert, Dr. Raymond Moore, is in full agreement. Dr. Moore suggests that children of less than seven or eight years are incapable of making moral judgments with consistency and accuracy; their inclination will be to do whatever they see other kids do, whether it be acceptable or not. He suggests that children under seven or eight be given only limited contact with peers, spending more time with one or both parents.

The impact of child-friends at the preschool level was recently examined by Dale Farran, a professor at the University of North Carolina. He compared 100 children who had been in a day-care situation from infancy through five with a control group of boys and girls who were not products of a day-care environment. The day-care children, who doubtless learned much from each other, were found to commit 15 times as many "aggressive acts" as the other children.

Farran emphasises that these children showed, "not just greater assertiveness or a willingness to stand up for one's rights," but also a tendency toward more *physical and verbal attacks on other children.*[21] There could be numerous reasons behind this, but one which cannot be avoided is that children are the world's greatest imitators. They do what they see being done.

How does this translate over to sibling problems in the home? I hope it's obvious. Children learn from their peers, whether in school, at the babysitter's, or down the street. It's entirely possible that one or more of your children are behaving with hostility just because they're seeing it done elsewhere. They use words, gestures, and facial expressions that they have seen others use with success. Try asking. Most kids will be more than happy to tell you exactly who it is they're copying!

We have a responsibility to expose our children to friends who will set good examples and to protect them from those who may undermine our work. It seems possible to reduce the effect other children have on our own children's behavior in two ways: (1) By providing them with Dr. Moore's "optimum early home background" to give them the solid values they need (and if you're past the early years, start *now* anyway!). (2) By limiting their contact with peers to those who are going to reinforce the values and character qualities you are teaching.

How can you guide your child's selection of friends without appearing to dominate? Be tactful and positive in your remarks. Control contact with a questionable peer by requiring, "If you're going to spend time with Matt I want it to be at our house, when Dad or Mom are home." If your children are still young enough to not be insisting on great privacy, make it your business to be in the same room—clipping coupons, reading, or doing something that allows you to keep your ears tuned to them. If they're playing outside, tend your garden, sweep the walk, or clean out the garage, but don't let them go unsupervised. When they reach the age of wanting to be "alone," give them some semblance of privacy, but try to remain within earshot. And don't let your children spend long times alone with kids you don't feel to be good for them—your instincts are probably right!

Use the times that your children are with their friends to reinforce the values you are teaching them. Proverbs warns us many times that certain people are capable of and bent on destroying close friendships. If you notice another child trying to destroy the relationship you are building between your children ("Let's go in the playhouse and lock your sister out."), take advantage of the teachable moment to work on team spirit. You may wish to respond with something like, "Susie, we don't allow our girls to treat each other that way, so please don't suggest that to Kathy." As you confirm in your children's minds exactly where the boundaries lie, you may be facing Susie with an idea she has never been asked to consider before. She may eventually refine a few values of her own, after having played with your children regularly under your loving supervision. If she should persist, however, gently send her home, reminding her that, "When we play here, we have to be kind. Maybe you can come back tomorrow."

We always encourage our children to play with their friends in *our* yard; that way we know what everyone is up to. Fortunately we have great neighbors; several families who seem to share our standards of behavior for kids. We parents have an unwritten agreement on how we handle these things, and we insist that we be told if our children misbehave at someone else's home. I have sent children home for getting into fistfights, and our boys have been sent home a time or two. But it doesn't happen often, because they know the boundaries, and they respect them.

Parents of preschoolers should monitor very closely any nursery care, playgrounds, preschools, or babysitting situations their children are in. If supervision isn't consistent, problems are certain to crop up.

Television

Television is an area which is daily requiring an increasing amount of "parental discretion" and limit-setting. We are realizing that just because something can be piped into a home and activated by a one-year-old doesn't mean it is fit for family viewing. Have you ever tried to get your child's attention while he is glued to the TV set? Have you noticed the tranquilized, mesmerized expression on his face in the midst of all that violence? Without unleashing a diatribe on the evils of the "boob-tube" and its influence on families, I will try to discuss only its effects on sibling conflicts.

According to the authors of *Teaching Television*, "Quarrels in many families revolve around program scheduling and time limits. Generally speaking, children can accept family rules if they are consistently enforced by parents and if the children are given constructive alternatives. For young children, the pressure of school friends should not override parents' better judgment.

"When a three-year-old prefers to watch *Sesame Street* and his eight-year-old brother wants to watch his favorite show, a problem is bound to arise as to who's 'Boss.' Parents can make it clear that there are certain times *each* child can watch TV and regularly limit those times so young children will grow up expecting such restrictions."[22]

A "good" television viewer must have the ability to separate fantasy from reality, since very little of what is seen on TV is real in the strictest sense. The so-called family viewing time contains more references to sex and many more suggestive innuendos than most family members would probably employ. The comedies that get the most laughs are those replete with snappy, insulting one-liners; on TV no one ever seems to suffer battered self-image, but in reality such remarks rarely hit their target without wounding.

We look at cartoon characters as the lightest of entertainment, unaware that a preschool-age child often sees those wild and wacky animals as extensions of himself—helpless, smaller than everyone else, and vulnerable. Nearly every cartoon problem is solved by physical violence. The little mouse clobbers a cat over the head with a baseball bat as a just reward for pulling his tail. Popeye beats Brutus to hamburger to win Olive Oyl's affection. Superheroes triumph over evil with a SLAM! BANG! POW! CRUNCH!

The authors of *Teaching Television* tell us such violence is significant:

> We find in our research that heavy viewing of cartoons leads to inappropriate and disruptive behavior among children in nursery school. Among our elementary school age children, the heavy car-

toon viewers were rated as unenthusiastic about school by their teacher.

Some parents have claimed that their children are quiet only when they watch TV. Thus, the parents particularly like Saturday morning, when the programs are geared to children. Most research, however, suggests that the very active child, or the child who gets into fights, becomes even more agitated by frequent TV viewing, especially when material involves cartoons, action-detective programs, or noisy game shows.[23]

We are told that by the time a child is 18, he has witnessed 18,000 murders on television, all in the name of entertainment. That's more than anyone would ever see in real life—even in the most crime-ridden inner-city district. A child who may be seeing more of the TV set than he is of his parents, receives a pretty big dose of non-reality.

One parent told me, "Our kids got hooked on the tube during summer vacation and I noticed a real increase in their physical violence toward one another. Where they used to be quite good at talking things over, they began hitting and hurting each other, sometimes resorting to some pretty mean stuff. Our three-year-old even overturned a bucket of water on his big sister's head! We talked to them about it and both admitted that they sometimes liked to pretend they were someone on TV. We suggested cutting back on their viewing time, and they didn't even complain. Now we limit it to more positive shows like *Sesame Street* and *Mister Rogers, Flipper* reruns and things like that. *They're doing a lot better.*"

If the television set has become your family altar and the *TV Guide* your daily devotional, it won't be easy to quit cold turkey. But you don't need to.

Begin by bringing it up at Family Time.* Ask the children if they have ever said or done something that they first heard or saw on TV. Then point out that, "Just like we won't let you run out into the street because we know it's not safe for you, we think you should

---

*Editor's note: An excellent guidebook for such discussion is *Making TV Work for Your Family* by William L. Coleman (Bethany House Publishers, 1983).

avoid certain TV programs that are not good for you. Can you think of reasons we might feel this way?" Wait for their response. Then, together, construct some suitable alternatives to the programming you think is negatively affecting your kids.

Because some fantasy is good for children, try having a story hour each night during which you read to the entire family. There are many great classics, including Christian fiction, which may be too difficult for some children to read alone, but would be received with great interest if read *to* them. Let the older children help by sharing in the reading. This will also serve to build and enhance their sibling relationship.

Try a family film night. Many public libraries have a large assortment of films, both educational and entertaining, that can be checked out with a projector and shown at your convenience. We periodically bring home a stack, pop a batch of popcorn, and have "movies." (Most recently we chose a Jiminy Cricket fire prevention film, a fantasy about kites, and a historical film on the Canadian mounties.) The list of titles available at our library is incredible.

Then, of course, there are always board games and card games that are a fun way to develop mental skills, unify the family, and create happy memories. You can probably come up with other ideas to distract your children from the magnetism of the silver tube. Try them for a couple of weeks and see if you like the results.

Here are the guidelines adopted by one family in their TV usage:[24]

1. Turn off the TV at mealtime; it's one of the few times the whole family is together and should be a time of positive communication.

2. Finish chores or homework before sitting down to watch TV.

3. Be selective in your choice of TV programming. Check TV listings before turning the set on. If nothing worthwhile is on, leave the TV off!

4. Use the TV to enhance your life, rather than allowing it to control your life. If you're scheduling your other weekly activities in order to watch a particular TV show, you're hooked!

5. Try to place your TV set where it's unobtrusive, yet arranged with your furniture in a way that encourages physical closeness during family viewing times.

6. Parents: Always make an effort to watch TV *with* your children. Talk about the programs you watch together. It's a great way to "tune in" to your children.

7. Consider TV viewing for your children as a privilege to be earned. Don't be afraid to lift the privilege as a disciplinary measure for poor grades or behavior.

8. If there's more than one child in the family, it's nice occasionally to invite one child at a time to stay up past the usual bedtime to watch a special program alone with Mom and Dad, to encourage one-to-one between parents and child.

9. Evaluate the amount of time you spend watching TV each week, and what you're watching. Then make a sincere effort to reduce the number of hours you're watching. Challenge yourself to turn off the TV and turn on family communication.

10. Consider giving up TV for a month at any time during the year. You'll find it a real challenge—and you may find out how hooked you really are.

Nutrition

This last "external" is a little more controversial. Some will read this section as they nod their heads knowingly and finish off with a hearty "amen!"—positive that they have seen behavior changes after their children have eaten certain foods. Others will read it and say, "Oh, come now, my kids can eat anything any time, and they always act the same way." Still others will skip these pages entirely, unwilling to admit that food may be causing some of their children's problems—or, at least unwilling to change things.

There is no doubt in my mind that many foods, eaten regularly by certain people, create adverse effects. Or that hunger can trigger violent behavior. I have seen it in myself and in our children, as well as in others. Most schoolteachers will affirm that food plays a vital role in the way children act. I think you will notice this also, if you will begin watching for it.

Dr. Lendon Smith is one of the most respected pediatricians of our day because of his theories that connect eating habits to specific behaviors. He has been telling parents for some time that people are exactly what they eat. In *Feed Your Kids Right*, Dr. Smith outlines a program of sensible eating designed to change the behavior that results from poor nutrition. He first advises parents to eliminate "antinutrients" from the family's diet. These "foods" actually *increase* the body's need for certain vitamins and minerals, rather than meeting any nutritional requirement on their own. The foremost antinutrient foods he attacks are sugar in all forms, refined carbohydrates, and artificial additives. All of these require B vitamins in order to be digested and metabolized, and none of them contain any. When the brown wheat germ is removed from whole wheat flour, the entire B complex of vitamins goes with it. When the flour is "enriched," a mere eight of the missing 22 nutrients are replaced—in minute quantities. Thus sugar, refined flour and grains, and additives must rob the body of those B vitamins destined for organs. Poor behavior is usually the first sign of such deficiency, and poor health is the inevitable final result.

Dr. Alan Cott relates that "in the treatment of 1,000 children suffering from behavior disorders or learning disabilities, I have found that a significant percentage were dramatically improved by removing sugar and other junk food from their diets. Those parents who were successful in enforcing the sugar-free diet achieved great success in helping their children overcome the hyperactive behavior that was interfering with their learning *and their peer relationships*." (Italics mine.)

He continues, "Most of the sweetened foods contain artificial colors and artificial flavors to which many children react with an allergy. [This] is not manifested in the usual ways but in a sudden outburst of disturbed, disruptive behavior produced by a reaction in the brain."[25]

I have always been bewildered by the TV commercial which shows a smiling, healthy, obviously "good" mother doling out snacks to her kids, and extolling a certain brand of "fresh, wholesome" (sugary, chocolaty, degermed, and creme-filled) cupcake because it "meets *my* tough standards." Yet, as one writer notes,

"Everything that is wrong with the American diet is rolled up in that [very same] snack cake or pie. . . . Encouraging a child—or his mother—to think of them as good nutrition is a little like teaching a four-year-old to smoke on the grounds that it will be good for his lungs."[26]

It is just as easy (and usually more economical) to offer your children frequent snacks of foods that are high in real food value. Apple slices, oranges, bananas, carrot sticks with a bowl of dip, raisins, nuts, cheese, little chunks of cooked/dried meat—all provide healthful eating without robbing the body of nutrients. Given a choice between sweets and non-sweets, most children will go for the sugary option. But if it's a choice between peanut butter on celery and nothing, kids will usually accept what's offered—and enjoy it.

We work vigorously to make our children aware of *why* eating right is important. I don't think Christopher ever tasted anything sweet, except fruit, until he was about two (Jonathan was a bit younger). We *have* to monitor every bite that goes into their mouths because of their extensive allergies. We therefore decided that the longer they didn't know about sweets the better off they'd be. So from the start we have been saying things such as, "That was nice of the lady to give us the pretty candy stick, but we won't eat it because it's made with lots of sugar, and sugar makes us act weird."

We are trying to create the same disdain for unhealthful foods that we hope they'll have for alcohol, tobacco, and harmful drugs. It hasn't been hard. One time I left Christopher with a friend and forgot to instruct her on his diet and tell her there were good things to eat in his bag. (It wasn't mealtime so I figured we were safe.) I picked him up a couple of hours later and he looked positively green. I asked him what was wrong and he replied, "I think I ate too many cookies. I don't feel very good in my tummy." I never did find out how many cookies he ate, but it didn't matter—they all came back up before we reached home. He still remembers that time, and has been careful to eat in moderation ever since.

Watch for physical or emotional reactions to other foods also. One friend of mine insists that tomatoes (in spaghetti, chili, catsup, and the like) will have her children bouncing off the walls. Another has a daughter who becomes moody and withdrawn when she eats chocolate. Our boys get hyped up on processed cheese (I suspect the artificial color is to blame). And when they do have sugar—well, I'd rather not describe it.

Become a label-reader who looks for "hidden" ingredients. If sugar is listed first or second in the list of ingredients, it's a major part of the product. If you don't see the word "sugar," look for sucrose (same thing), dextrose, corn syrup, corn sweeteners, or brown sugar (it's no more healthful than white). You will be amazed at all the foods that contain sugar for no apparent reason. Catsup, salad dressings, many soups and seasoning mixes, and bread are a few that have surprised me. Even an apparently harmless stick of chewing gum contains a half-teaspoon of sugar. A 12-ounce soft drink has nine teaspoons, and two cups of fruit cocktail will give your family 14 teaspoons of sugar. "Ades" and "fruit drinks" are misleading. When the makers tell you it contains "10% real fruit juice," they are really telling you the beverage is 90% water, sugar, artificial flavors and colors. And the popular breakfast drink that "people like better than orange juice" will start your children off with a whopping 12 teaspoons of sugar per 8-ounce glass.

A word of caution: do not select foods just because they are labeled "natural." This word is used on everything these days, and sugar is frequently one of the first "natural" ingredients listed on the side panel.

Low blood sugar is a malady which sounds as if it could be corrected by ingesting *more* sugar. Paradoxically, this is false. Low blood sugar stems from an overproduction of insulin, which has been triggered by eating sugar or refined carbohydrates. The result of this condition, says Dr. Alan Cott, is "overactive and at times violent behavior."[27] To keep blood sugar level normal and behavior predictable, encourage frequent snacking—on nourishing foods. There is nothing wrong with eating something light (a handful of nuts, a half an apple, or a glass of juice) every hour or two, but you should then scale down the daily three meals to a size in keeping with those nutritious snacks.

My first great failure to keep Christopher's blood sugar level moderated came when he was about two. My sister was getting married and we had no qualms about letting him sit with us in the front row at her wedding—he rarely misbehaved. At four p.m. we awakened him from a three-hour nap and hopped into the car for the half-hour trip. Upon arriving at the church, we busied ourselves with preparations. At six o'clock I took up my station behind the guest book, Ralph began ushering people down the aisle, and Christopher began crying. Every little thing that happened evoked a new outburst of tears. I pleaded, begged, threatened, bribed. I was desperate for this wedding to be lovely. During the ceremony he started up again. My mother rummaged in her purse, looking for something to interest him—no luck. At last, after the 20-minute service had seemingly dragged on for two hours, we were dismissed to the reception hall. As we entered the room, Christopher galloped across the bare floor, straight for the refreshment table, and grabbed a *huge* handful of nuts. He was hungry! It then occurred to me for the very first time, *This kid hasn't eaten since lunch time, and it's nearly eight p.m. How could I do such a thing?* I don't know if my sister has forgiven me for disrupting her wedding, but I certainly learned a valuable lesson. Now, before we go anywhere, we make sure the boys have eaten something high in protein and healthful; and if it's going to be a long outing, we take plenty of munchies with us.

Dr. Smith says, "If one can banish antinutrients and get the whole family on a program of sound nutrition, within three or four weeks everybody should feel better and be more cheerful. . . . Persistent rashes and watery noses should clear up. Head- and stomach-aches should be gone or only mild. Tempers will not flare so easily. It is important that the whole family follow good eating habits. If Father still puts sugar in his coffee and has a piece of pie for dessert in front of the five-year-old who loves pie but gets six grapes and a piece of cheese instead, the program will break down."[28]

For many families, it would be unthinkable to make all these changes at one time. Therefore, try making one alteration a month. For example, if your children are hooked on the sugar-coated junkies for breakfast fare, begin giving them peanut butter or grilled cheese sandwiches (or something more conventional such as eggs, or oatmeal sweetened with applesauce), then give them sweet cereal in the evening, after a good dinner, as a dessert. Or make a simple change from white bread to whole wheat bread. Or from soft drinks to fruit juice. And take careful notice of any changes that occur—good or bad—in your kids' behavior.

Lendon Smith reminds us that "nutrition seems basic to the development of the mature human. If a child is a crabby, surly, touchy, noncompliant animal all the time, he may be suffering from worms, anemia, or odd brain waves. If his behavior is inconsistent and could be classified as "emotionally unstable" (Jekyll and Hyde), then it would be worth noting what foods were ingested in the one to twelve hours prior to the particular outburst."[29]

One mother underscored this beautifully with these comments: "Many times a 'fight' occurs because the children are hungry and Mother's reaction is not as patient as it could be because she is tired and hungry also. Quick protein snacks are a big help. Perhaps an earlier meal would help. Halloween is a prime time for tears and fights because of the candy. We are what we eat—and it certainly shows up in children."

Other factors that affect behavior are oncoming illness and the need for sleep. If one of your children is acting cranky and irritable, consider that he might need a nap, or an earlier bedtime. If the child has, without a doubt, gotten all the sleep he could possibly need, don't be surprised if within twenty-four hours he shows signs of illness.

One of our sons is just as predictable as Big Ben in this respect. If he has a whiney, ornery, rotten day, I know he's catching a cold that hasn't shown up yet. He's never failed me yet. A child in this condition should be kept away from brothers and sisters as much as possible, not so much to check the spreading of the illness as to keep him from spreading *trouble*. Try to involve a difficult child in something you are doing, even if it's just sitting on a stool in the kitchen while watching you prepare dinner. A physical or emotional need behind a "bad day" can often be alleviated by closeness with a parent. That's one thing you'll never want to limit!

114

Parent Talk

Discuss: Do our children have any friends or outside influences which are affecting how they treat one another? What could we as parents do to achieve a little more control of such situations?

Family Time

1. Conduct a family discussion of boundaries. Point out limits imposed by things around the house, asking questions such as, "Why do we have a fence around the yard?" (to keep the dog in), or "Why do we have to have a door on the refrigerator?" (to keep the cold air from escaping). Ask, "Why are limits necessary?"
2. Discuss with your children things that may have an adverse effect on their behavior—diet, TV violence, peers who set a bad example or encourage them to do wrong. Decide together what types of limits should be set (the children will usually be quite reasonable).

11

Helping a Child
"Move Over"—Happily!

The best way to prevent much sibling rivalry is adequate preparation *before* a sibling ever arrives on the scene. Adequate prevention can make the arrival of a new baby as untraumatic as possible for everyone involved.

The most important sales pitch you will ever have to give is the one to convince your older child that having a new child in the family will be to his advantage. Unlike the vacuum cleaner saleman's pitch, which can be finished within an hour, yours will take considerably longer—at least nine months!

Consider the plight of the toddler. Normally he is not consulted in his parents' decision to have another child, and he is satisfied with things the way they are. But while not being a party to the decision, he has certainly been a *factor* in it. Do any of the following sound familiar?

"My, what a *big* boy—you're sure not a baby anymore."

"Remember how cute Jason was when he was that age?"

"She's almost two—she *needs* a brother or sister."

Frequently the child is on the threshold of the "terrible twos"

when the parents get that urge to cuddle another bundle of inno-
cence. However, the two-year-old has a mind of his own. And he
hasn't yet learned the arithmetic of love—that it multiplies as the
family grows. A young child sees a new baby as competition, as an
indication that his parents aren't satisfied with the "old." In reality,
though, we know that this is almost never the case; but try explain-
ing that to a rambunctious one-, two-, or three-year-old who is constantly being told, "No, don't do that," "Please be quiet," "Sit still,"
"Go away," and "Why didn't you use the potty?"

Consider this: if your spouse ever came home and told you that
he'd enjoyed being married to you so much that he had decided to
take an *additional* spouse, you would be crushed!

Here are a few suggestions that may help make the transition in
your home a little easier:

1. *Begin talking about a baby even before pregnancy* if you are
considering having another child. Say such things as, "Wouldn't it
be nice if God would let us have a baby brother or sister for our family?" and "I bet you'd be a very kind big brother if we had a baby
around here."

2. *Avoid the term "new."* When your daughter gets a new
toothbrush, what do you do with the old one? When you buy your
son new boots, it is usually because the old ones are too ragged to
wear and will be thrown out. When you take down a new box of cereal, does everyone clamor for the old? Or the new?

In a child's mind, older is not necessarily better. New bikes are
shiny, old ones are junky; new shoes are colorful, old ones are
scuffed. Have a *little* baby, *another* baby, a *tiny* baby—but don't
have a *new* baby. Make sure, too, that your child knows he or she
will retain his value as a member of the household—*tell* him. More
than one child has been distressed at the idea that, like Dad's old
Chevy, he was being traded in for a "new model."

3. *Point out friends among his peers who have babies in their
families.* "Donny is probably so happy to have a baby sister," or "I
hear that Kimmy really likes to help with their baby," might be good
ways to discuss this.

Whether you're "planning" a new addition or not, try to keep your comments about babies and small children positive. Don't say, "I sure feel sorry for Valerie's mom, having a baby with colic. She looks exhausted all the time." Rather, if you must say anything at all, try, "David's sister is growing up so fast; she should be sleeping better in no time." If your child sees in your attitude a reverence for God's creative masterpieces, an appreciation for even the tiniest and most helpless human being, he will adopt a similar attitude. If, perchance, another child does arrive, your earlier child will be better prepared. If one does not arrive, he will at least be a more sensitive and appreciative parent someday, as a result of your programming.

4. *When talking with your child about the upcoming arrival, try to focus on his role rather than the baby's.* My mother has been very clever about this anytime a new grandchild is expected. Before Timothy's recent birth she would often say to Jonathan, "My won't you be BIG when you're big enough to be a big brother!" That was much preferable to "Won't it be exciting when the new baby comes?" (which is probably what I would have said).

5. *Don't promise what you can't deliver.* Don't tell your child that he is going to get a new playmate who will be lots of fun. Tiny babies are never very good playmates for displaced siblings. It's also best not to tell the child that "it will be *your* baby." Some kids have used this as license to destroy. Always refer to *our* baby—a part of the team. An older child may have a doll as his baby, though, and can imitate and learn valuable parenting skills from you by playing with it.

If your child has his heart set on a sister or a brother, try to prepare him for the law of averages—about half the people who want a baby of a certain sex will be disappointed. If Susie is declaring she wants a little brother this time, you might say, "A boy would be fun, but if we had another girl we could make you dresses just alike. That would be fun, too!" Or, in the opposite case, "It would be nice to have a little girl, but if we get a boy we would know that God thought we needed a brother to liven up the place a little." Many times, if parents show no partiality, and if the suggestion isn't made that a child should wish for one or the other, the idea won't even occur to him.

You can add to the suspense of the preparation by saying from the very beginning, "God already knows if this is a boy or a girl. He knows what our family needs most right now, and He's already decided. Won't it be exciting to see which He surprises us with? It will be almost like opening a birthday present."

6. Whenever possible, opt for family-centered maternity care, to ease the new child into the family gently. Many hospitals now offer sibling visiting hours and short stays for healthy mothers and babies. Some parents also elect to have birth-center deliveries or home births, so there is not a lengthy separation of the parents from the other children. Some experts now believe that siblings have the same potential for "bonding" with a new baby that the parents have, but of course only if they are given the chance. Childbirth options are discussed in greater detail in *The Natural Childbirth Book*.

7. After the baby is born, coach the child concerning the infant's statistics, such as his name and his weight. Then, when people stop and inquire, say, "Jeremy can tell you that, can't you, honey?"

8. Stock up on inexpensive little items and wrap them up as gifts for your child to open when people offer gifts for the baby. The items will depend on the age and interest of the older child, but we had great success with a few Matchbox cars and some "big brother" clothes—white T-shirts, a belt with a real buckle, and new cowboy boots.

When Jonathan was born, we were even able to have a party. Since we had planned a medically-attended home birth, it was easy to begin the festivities the very night our baby arrived. After all, we reasoned, if all the other birthdays are usually celebrated, why not the initial birth day? I baked a cake ahead of time and froze it, already decorated with "Welcome Baby." When I went into labor we took the cake out, and later that night we ate it!

I felt very good after the delivery, so Christopher was able to see that having a baby wasn't traumatic for any of us. And we were all able to remain together. The only difference was that the baby was now "out" instead of "in." Our older son opened his "big brother" presents that night, along with a card that said, "Thank you for being my brother. I think I'm going to like it here. Love, Jonathan." We had also wrapped a couple of token gifts for the newcomer (since it was *his* birthday), but he slept through the festivities. We did the same thing for both the older boys after Timothy was born. They took great delight in the celebration itself, but even more in preparing for it ahead of time. We made a cake to freeze, bought balloons, and decorated our own plates and napkins. If a hospital birth occurred, parents could easily stage such a party as a homecoming celebration. Everyone loves a party! Just be sure the work is done in advance, so it's not a big hassle for a mother who should be taking it easy. Shopping trips, cake-baking, non-family guests, and any other related inherent stresses are absolute no-nos for recuperating moms.

9. Encourage your older child to do things with the baby, such as holding a shiny toy within his grasp or putting his booties on. Say things whenever you can to point out that their relationship is growing—for example, "See how you made him laugh when you played peek-a-boo? I can tell he really likes you." Stress the right way to do things rather than the wrong. Say, "That's right, be very gentle with a tiny baby," not, "Look out—you're going to hurt him!"

10. I'm a firm believer in the Golden Rule. Give a friend's older child the same consideration you hope people will have for yours. I am still often tempted to dash up to a friend and ogle an adorable new infant, but usually, if I slow down enough to gaze knee-level, I'll find myself staring into the eyes of a somber-faced toddler who is clutching Mama's skirt. As hard as he is to notice at such a time, try speaking to the toddler first, even before you greet the parents. Inquire about him, rather than asking, "Is that your little baby sister?" Give him those few moments, and you'll be doing those parents a huge favor, which may someday be returned to you.

You might try sending the cards of congratulations to the baby's sibling instead of his parents. And whenever you have a new baby gift, wrap something up for the older child too. He will appreciate the thought almost as much as his parents.

Let me remind you that even the most thorough preparation will not help if you neglect to maintain your home's atmosphere over the years. Preparation is important, but it is not the only answer. No matter what ages your children are, you can change and control the environment. It's not hopeless!

12

Starting in Midstream

No doubt some readers are thinking, *What you say seems to be geared more to families with children younger than ours. Our kids are older and more set in their ways. Is there any hope for people like us?* I believe there is.

Up to this point we have stressed repeatedly the concepts of prevention and dealing with problems while children are young; after all, parents wield more influence over the development of attitudes and habits while their children are still young and pliable. As the children grow older, they, as all of us, begin to "gel," to become that final product that has been forming all these years.

Young children are, as Anne Ortlund says, "wet cement," bearing for a lifetime those impressions of the early years. But they are not exactly like wet cement, for they possess a soul and spirit, an increasingly logical mind, and the abilities to speak, understand, and communicate.

If your children are still fairly young (under age six), count yourself blessed! There is still plenty of time, if you begin today, to incorporate into your family life the atmospheric changes we have been talking about. With careful, creative management of your many opportunities, you will see results.

Children of grade-school age still have great potential. Between six and eleven, they have an enormous desire to cooperate, and they especially love challenges. The atmospheric changes are still the first step, but you will notice additional positive results if you make the changing process a game for them. Charts, points, and rewards may accomplish amazing things in children in this age group. (This matter is discussed more thoroughly in chapter 13.)

Even parents of teenagers have hope, insists Dan Davidson, a pastor, father, and family counselor who is particularly gifted in helping people deal with relationships. Dr. Davidson admits that the best time to instill lasting habits and character traits is while children are small. However, he offers two steps that should be taken by a parent of older children who feels the need for a fresh start.

First, *identify the problem.* Hopefully both parents will agree that a problem exists and on what it is. They should be as specific as possible. Don't say, "Sandy and Mark don't seem to want anything to do with each other." Rather, say, "Sandy seems to resent having to drive Mark to school each day. She shows it by calling him demeaning names every time she sees him. Mark retaliates by playing practical jokes which embarrass her." Upon arriving at the problem, parents should seek God's guidance in presenting it to the children in a tactful, healthy manner. The second step, *Bring the family together and establish the following:*

A. *That a problem exists.* Do not begin by recounting the most recent battle or allowing them to do so. It's *your* turn to talk. You might begin by saying, "Kids, tonight Mom and I want to talk to you about something that's bothering us. We want you to hear us out. No one is to say anything until asked. Is that understood? Good.

"We are becoming quite disturbed by the amount of bickering and name-calling that's going on between you. It doesn't strike us as being a good way of handling disagreements, no matter who's at fault. We have failed you in not stopping this conduct before now, but we have seen our error and want to straighten things out. We are a Christian family, and we need to prove to ourselves, if to no one else, that the Christian life works for us."

B. *Family devotions.* If this has not been a regular part of your lives before, expect a little resistance. But there may be less resistance if you don't call it "family altar" or "devotions." You might say instead, "We've decided that as a family we're going to take a few minutes each evening after supper to read the Bible together. We believe that God has answers in it for us—do you?" Then read something appropriate.

C. *Family conference.* This will be a time and place where grievances are aired and solutions discussed. The idea of a family conference may be new to many, but once the ground rules are laid it can be a marvelous tool. You could say, "We are going to begin meeting once a week, to talk about our family and work out our problems. You kids are getting old enough that you don't need to carry on like the Hatfields and McCoys. From now on, we don't want you arguing among yourselves. Instead, write down your problems and bring them to the next family conference. We'll discuss them then." (Many disputes will have a way of working themselves out while they're waiting for conference time.) One mother of *eleven* noted that the family conference works best in small families. Therefore, if one has several children, a direct confrontation involving only those people who seem to be having trouble is more appropriate. No one wants personal difficulties aired "in public."

D. *Ground rules.* If trouble has been brewing for some time, your children have had a chance to become quite creative and cunning in the tortures they dream up for one another. You must ferret out every possible source of friction, then make some rules to forestall any future confrontations. Now is the time to let your teens speak up, to let you know what's bothering them. It should not turn into a shouting match—be sure you stay in control of the meeting. You may wish to draw guidelines about name-calling, teasing, household responsibilities, telephone use, conduct with friends, or whatever the problems seem to stem from. After setting up the ground rules, establish a workable plan for enforcement, and some reasonable consequences for violations.

E. *A Family contract.* Obtain a notebook specifically for this purpose and have your children write out the rules and the enforcement procedures, just the ways laws are recorded at the seats of government. Dr. Davidson believes this will help your children see the concepts and character qualities for which they now are going to consciously strive. He recommends the following format for the family contract:

1. We will discuss all disputes with our parents. This will not be at mealtime or any other spontaneous time. We will meet each _____ at _____ o'clock, or whenever a meeting is called by our parents.
2. We will follow these scriptural steps for handling disagreements. (Have the children themselves look these up and write them in the book.)
   a. Matthew 18:15 _____
   b. Luke 17:3, 4 _____
   c. Galatians 6:1 _____
   d. Matthew 5:23, 24 _____
3. We will practice RESISTANCE (not yielding to the temptation to say or do something spiteful) and RESTRAINT (if we catch ourselves after yielding to a temptation, we will stop—IMMEDIATELY!).
4. When we feel negative emotions toward other family members, we agree to enlist the help of Mom and Dad. Our parents agree to keep these discussions confidential, and try to help rather than condemn.

Signed: _____

_____

The key, says Dr. Davidson, is for the young people to be made sensitive to the problem. Each must admit that a change is needed before the changes can progress.

What should parents do if an older child is in the midst of an obvious period of rebellion and does not seem sensitive to much of anything important? Dr. Davidson suggests it is then the parents' duty to present an ultimatum. They might approach the child with, "Regardless of whether or not you agree with the reasons we have for all this, it's necessary for all people to learn acceptable ways of getting along with others. We have wronged you by not insisting long ago that your behavior stop. We ask your forgiveness, but we need to start out together, in step. You are just ＿＿ short years from legal adulthood. Adults cannot get by with treating others the way you treat Rachel. We can no longer allow this behavior, because the Bible warns us that 'a kind man benefits himself, but a cruel man brings himself harm' (Prov. 11:17). We love you too much to let you hurt yourself by hurting others, so you'll have to live by the house rules—or else!"

Or else what? You be the judge of that. You know your teenager and what will motivate him. It is possible that when your child sees the limits you have set and is aware that you mean business, he will give cooperation a whirl. You will not lose anything by a conversation like this. But you do have much to gain.

Parent Talk

1. To what extent have we already been dealing with our children's sibling difficulties?
2. Discuss: Are there any areas of sibling problems that will require a large degree of improvement?
3. If you feel a Family Conference Table would benefit your family, establish one today, as described in this chapter.

Family Time

Write each family member's name on a slip of paper, then have each person draw the name of a "secret pal." Each day, for a week, a secret pal should think of two kind things to do *in secret* for that person each day (e.g., putting away his clean laundry, leaving an apple on his dresser, doing one of his chores before he gets the chance). At the end of the week, have the secret pals reveal their identities.

13

Waiting for the Good Fruit

A large shade tree in our front yard became firewood not long ago. The reason? Rotted roots. Some city maintenance men came one day to repair our sidewalk, and in the process had to unearth one of the tree's roots which was causing the walk to bulge. They showed me a section of the root—a slimy, gray mass which convinced me that we had found the reason why, in the middle of summer, the tree had no leaves.

We've compared children's behavior to the fruit on a tree, stressing that until the *root* problems are discovered and corrected, it will be difficult to deal with the fruit. Once the roots are cured, healthier fruit, or behavior, will result. However, this doesn't usually happen overnight, and many parents may have a hard time coping while waiting for the good fruit to appear. This chapter is dedicated to "pruning"—dealing with unacceptable behavior as it appears, gently removing it to make room for the fruit of the Spirit.

The following suggestions are really not solutions in themselves. At best, they are temporary measures to deal with rough spots in the parenting journey. The goal is to have all the children, as well as their parents, tuned in to God's will, walking in obedience to the Holy

Spirit. "If we walk in the light, as he is in the light, *we have fellow-ship with one another*, and the blood of Jesus, his Son, purifies us from all sin" (1 John 1:7). Children cannot be expected to be born knowing this, but they are capable of learning it, and they will, if our training is focused toward that ideal. Meanwhile, here are suggestions from seasoned parents on how to curtail the conflicts that inevitably take place during the learning period.

Rewards

Most children fight more if they are confined together in the same house, car, or room for a long time. For this reason, parents must use strategy to keep quarrels to a minimum—and to remain sane. The easiest and most logical strategy is to make good behavior *profitable*.

As I write this I am sitting in a park on a Saturday, watching our boys romp and play with nearly thirty other youngsters, most of whom are accompanied by one or both parents. I am wondering how many of those parents earlier used this outing to motivate their children toward some desired behavior. I don't mind admitting that I did. This trip is part of a rewards system we employ regularly to reinforce habits of pleasantness in our children.

Since my husband frequently has to work on school holidays and Saturdays, I am often left alone to find constructive, interesting activities to break up those long days and help them move faster and more smoothly. We often reward an hour's fight-free play with a story-reading time or a treat of some sort. Today I was trying desperately to get the house in order for evening guests. The boys kept thwarting my efforts by finding things to disagree about, thus requiring my intervention. After considering the possible causes for their behavior. I decided they were probably just bored and needed a change of scenery. So I made an offer.

"Boys, I'll make a deal with you. I need about one hour to be left alone so I can put the house in order. Then we may have some fun together. If you guys can play outside for just one hour without tattling, arguing, teasing, fighting, or anything else that requires my attention, we'll walk to the park when I'm done vacuuming. *But*—if you do any of those things, whoever's involved will come in and take a nap, and there'll be no trip to the park for anyone. Do we have a deal?" (Of course we did!) "Good. I'll set the timer."

The purpose of giving rewards is to develop patterns of behavior that we want to see consistently. Businesses use rewards and call them "incentives"; they offer bonuses, gifts, and fringe benefits to employees who are the most productive. Teachers reward academic progress with good grades. Most child-rearing authorities believe that rewarding *good* behavior works much better in the long run than punishing bad conduct. Here are a few guidelines for developing a reward system that fits your family's needs.

1. Keep the benefits simple but desirable. Rewards should be fun to anticipate, but should not become forms of bribery or blackmail. Offer simple favors, like getting to stay up an extra half-hour or being allowed to choose the main course for supper. Some parents make up charts and have their children accumulate points, stars, or stickers toward something special in the future. (Remember when stores gave savings stamps so we'd be sure and shop there?)

2. Just as the rewards are simple, so should be the method of earning them. Focus on one area of behavior at a time. Giving a child too many instructions at once usually results in frustration for everyone. Try beginning with a chart of "attitudes" as suggested in Dobson's *Dare to Discipline.* Or perhaps, as Mike and Judy Phillips have done, offer something such as a peanut each time a child uses "courtesy words" or shares a toy without being asked. Resist the impulse to give big rewards, even if your kids do make you extremely proud. You'll never be able to afford to keep it up, and they'll end up expecting to be paid for everything.

3. Have variety to maintain interest. After two to four weeks with one method, try a new chart or another plan. Ever wonder why your grocery store has three to six different contests per year, instead of just one? Variety. It's the spice of life, you know.

4. As you see the desired behavior becoming more and more habitual, taper off the rewards. The rewards are *temporary* measures used to instill new, enduring habits.

5. Don't forget encouragement and praise. Often the warmth in your eyes and the pride in your voice are enough to make a child want to repeat good behavior.

6. Be consistent and fair. If your children see that you're trying to be fair, they will be more tolerant and understanding of those occasional mistakes that every parent makes. When an incentive plan is not received with enthusiasm, the problem may stem from inconsistency in some previous effort. Check that possibility out; kids know if you follow through on your promises.

Conflicts Over Possessions

Most parents would love having a sure-fire method of preventing their kids from fighting over what belongs to whom. While I'm sure there's no perfect answer, many problems can be eliminated by marking items with a certain color, initial, or symbol as soon as they enter your home. This takes that four-letter-word, *time*, but it will pay dividends of peace and quiet that make it worthwhile.

Most homes have a large number of toys and other items that are "community property." In fact, in our home, most of the items therein eventually fall into that category. But, on the theory that one can't very well give away something that doesn't belong to him, I believe children need to experience some private ownership in order to learn the full joy of giving and sharing.

When a toy is new and its ownership definite, and while the interest in the toy is high, the real owner should be entitled to control its use. For this reason, each of our boys has a drawer for keeping "special" things that are not quite ready for the usual treatment. After that initial round of strict possession, when I usually find the item abandoned somewhere, I then consign it to the regular toy area, where anyone can play with it. Of course it actually still belongs to the original owner, but we've found he isn't too picky after a while.

Some parents minimize the ownership problem by not buying things that are different enough to be compared. At Christmas, for example, they may try to equalize things on a dollar basis, but even then, one gift seems to have more pizazz than another. To avoid this, rather than giving the race-car set the son wants and the cassette re-corder the daughter has asked for, why not make them community gifts so the whole family can enjoy them?

A kitchen timer is a great instrument for insuring fair use of possessions. Set it for brief intervals and the kids will usually take turns happily, knowing that justice prevails. Besides, I've never seen kids go through more than two turns apiece at something before someone loses interest and moves on to something else.

Families with teens may wish to keep (along with the "family contract") a written record of who borrows what and when it is returned. The house rule should be, of course, "Use another's things *only* with permission."

If conflicts repeatedly erupt over items which have no clear ownership, taking away the object for a while seems the best way to soften everyone's heart. Even very young children may decide it's better to take turns than to lose out entirely. Older children might be called to sit at a "bargaining table" and reach a decision themselves, with the condition that the item will be returned only after they agree upon a solution.

Other Causes of Conflict

Many of life's smallest conflicts emit the most noise—such as when two children both decide they want the same twelve-inch segment of the eight-foot couch. The most equitable solution here seems to be the "Great Wall"—a blanket, pillow, or length of masking tape used to physically divide the controversial space. Masking tape can also divide the car's backseat into three equal parts, if that's what you need, but give the child in the middle a few extra inches for the inconvenience of not having a window.

If glasses of juice or pieces of pie are being given to two exacting youngsters, let one child do the dividing and the other one have first choice.

Sometimes physical violence results from pent-up energy that needs to be channeled. Be sure the kids are able to run and exercise every day. If they begin harassing each other, send them for a few laps around the yard, a bike ride, or some push ups. Housebound? We purchased a mini-trampoline for rainy indoor days. It's about three feet in diameter and stores under a bed. When the boys get rowdy, we prescribe 40 bounces.

Some children argue and bicker out of boredom—they need a change of scenery. This does not mean that we parents need to be on call to entertain them twenty-four hours a day, but rather that we should keep the surroundings interesting and challenging. Watch as your children's interests expand, and try to think of ways you can help them grow. Introduce them to the wonders of the library. Help them find classes and clubs that will widen their horizons. If they show a love for music, try with all your might to provide an instrument and lessons. Discover what interests your child's friends; it may be something which your own child finds intriguing but hasn't yet mastered.

I try to plan at least one interesting activity to do with our sons every day. It may be a trip to the library or a mall, it may be baking together, or roller skating around the neighborhood in a funny little parade, or visiting a special friend or neighbor. When they have something to look forward to, it seems to make the day a little brighter and everyone's outlook is a little more cheery.

Many times a conflict will start out on a small scale, but human nature and pride being what they are, both parties find it difficult to back down without losing face. Parents have therefore invented all sorts of ways to break up verbal exchanges without having to declare a winner or loser. A pastor's wife I know would take two bickering children and make them stand at opposite ends of the room. She then had them take turns stepping toward one another until they were nose to nose. Usually by this time they were convulsing with giggles, knowing what was going to happen next. Finally, they had to *hug* each other, and if they'd been especially difficult, *kiss* as well.

Another mother parks her two children in two chairs about three feet apart and makes them face each other until they can make one another smile. Because of the nature of children to clown and cut up, this usually takes no time at all.

Or try a "crabby party." Pull up a circle of chairs (one for you, too!) and announce, "All right, we're all going to sit here and be grouchy for five minutes. No one will be allowed to smile—we'll get it all over with at once." Everyone should be snickering within a minute or two.

At least one mother (my own) was able to stop her teenage daughters' cat fights by tape recording them (in secret) and replaying the argument for them later. We became much more careful about what we said!

The purpose of these gimmicks is to take the focus off the dispute at hand and show our children how silly it is to quarrel over little things. These techniques do not place blame, but they do restore peace. Perhaps the most effective tool is isolation. It is very simple to say, "You two don't seem to be having much fun together today. Let's call a time-out and have each of you play in separate rooms for a while." Kids often just want to be alone.

Consequences

Sometimes a child or group of children just won't respond to rewards. For these it may be necessary to develop some fitting consequences to encourage them to bear the responsibility for their battles. I have found two creative ways parents have done this. (Once you get the idea you'll probably think of many others!)

One family makes a weekly chart for each child with eight spaces numbered from the bottom up (see next page). The top four spaces list privileges or activities the children especially enjoy. They are told, "Every time we parents have to intervene in one of your disputes this week, we will mark a number off your chart. You will get four chances, but after that, each fight will cost you something fun." These parents consistently mark the charts and enforce the ground rules. They tell me their children are much more eager to work things out between themselves than they used to be.

Another mother kept a small jar for each child, filling it with $1.00 in nickels at the beginning of each week. Any time she discovered full-scale trouble she would remove one nickel from each offender's jar. At the end of the week, the children received whatever money remained in their jars. That's an effective combination of rewards *and* consequences!

Billy	*Nancy*
8. Cookout at Gram's	8. Cookout at Gram's
7. Trip to Swap Meet	7. Overnight at Debbie's
6. Swimming on Saturday	6. Shopping for fabric with Mom
5. 1 hour of TV (parents' choice)	5. 1 hour of TV (parents' choice)
4.	4.
3.	3.
2.	✗ 9-18-83
✗ 9-16-83	✗ 9-16-83

Tattling

A friend of mine once lamented, "I hope this summer isn't like last year. I don't mind the fact that the house seems to be crawling with kids, but *I can't stand the tattling!*"

Tattling is sometimes hard to cope with because, while one half of our being wants to tune it out, another side feels compelled to at least hear the talebearer out. After all, a child sometimes reports things we need to know and would have missed otherwise. And he needs to know we are concerned about what goes on. But if he is tattling, he must be dealt with.

Like all other forms of childish misbehavior, tattling usually has root causes. I am reminded of an incident that occurred when I had a much narrower view of the subject. A friend, Dona, and I were feeling ambitious one day while she was at my house, so we not only baked and decorated a carrot cake for supper that night, but we decided to throw a badly-needed coat of paint on the walls of one bedroom. Of course that sounds easier than it actually was, because our four young sons were also wanting to help, if able to get near the project. For their sakes, we propped a baby gate in the doorway of the bedroom and got them settled happily right outside the window, playing in the backyard. But it seemed that about every five minutes or less, somebody would come to the gate to "tell" on someone for doing something wrong.

One boy (mine) was coming very frequently—I felt like painting his face the next time he appeared. After about the tenth episode of tattling, I took down the gate, went outside, and gathered the boys around me. "Boys," I began, "we've heard enough tattling for one day now. You guys need to work out some of your own problems. The only time it's right to 'tell' on someone is if they're doing something dangerous. If they're just bothering you, get away and find something else to do. We are *tired* of tattling—do you understand?"

"Yes," they repeated in unison.

"When is the only time you may tell on someone?"

"When it's *dangerous*," they chorused.

"Good! Let's see if we can do better. Dona and I will be finished pretty soon."

Peace ensued. In fact, things became so quiet that we wondered what the kids were up to, but an occasional giggle and a few muffled words convinced us that they were now in the house and apparently getting along as the good friends they were.

As we were climbing down the ladder for the last time, feeling rather pleased with accomplishments, my son came and stood silently at the gate. I complimented him on his great job of spending an entire hour without acting as town crier, then added, "What's everyone been doing, anyway?"

"Oh, not much. Just finishing off the carrot cake."

Dona could have won a prize for her graceful leap over the baby gate, but she was too late. The cake had been devoured. Foolishly, I asked my son why he had not told us what was going on. His reply was predictable: "I didn't think it was *dangerous*."

One frequent motive for excessive tattling is the desire to get attention. Dona and I were preoccupied with our painting that day, and our children were probably aware that they weren't going to get much attention by behaving well. But a tattletale would have an audience, at least for a moment or two.

Some children tattle because their sense of justice can't tolerate wrongs going by unnoticed, and they want the security of knowing that the person in charge is aware of what is happening. We need to recognize these yearnings in children and deal with them. Of course, some tattle just to antagonize each other.

A preschool director has come up with some creative responses to those tiring tales, theorizing that children often "tell" because they think the adult in charge missed seeing something. (We adults are supposed to be all-knowing and ever-present, remember?) She suggests that a simple acknowledgment such as "You wanted me to know that" will frequently satisfy. What you are doing in that case, instead of becoming involved in the dispute, is to recognize what the tattler must be feeling and voice that recognition.

When I tried my own version of this response on our children and a few neighbors, I was amazed to find it worked! Whenever someone came running to me with a report of something insignificant, I replied, "I see. Thanks for letting me know." In every instance the child immediately returned to his play. This showed me that often kids are not really asking us to intervene or provide solutions as much as they are reinforcing in their own minds that someone cares about what is taking place. They hope you will want to know about life's small injustices.

A clever kindergarten teacher handled these occasions a bit differently. She made a large yarn "tattle-tail" and carried it around the playground with her. Her intention was to pin it to the next child who tattled; but as you might guess, she never got to do it—the kids quit "telling."

Instigators

The very worst kind of tattling, and the kind we should squelch at all costs, is that which smacks of "instigatorism"—done for the sole satisfaction of seeing another child get into trouble.

The Bible warns us to "watch out for those who cause division" (Rom. 16:17). An instigator, by my definition, is a child who is adept at conveniently managing to get the other kids into trouble while he appears to remain uninvolved. This child often stirs trouble between two other siblings by reporting their deeds back and forth until war breaks out, then says to Mom or Dad, "I'm trying to do my homework, but Chad and Jason are making too much noise with their fighting."

Sometimes an instigator will covertly display his hostility toward a sibling by encouraging him to do something for which he will certainly get punished, then making sure the appropriate authority finds out about it.

Detecting an instigator is not always easy, but try the kid who seems to be wearing a halo. (Remember Sidney in *The Adventures of Tom Sawyer*?) A very subtle type of troublemaker is the child who happens to outshine his brother or sister in behavior or achievements, then sets up a comparison situation that is hard to ignore. Try to keep your astonishment at the near-perfection of "Sidney" to a minimum—he's got you fooled.

Parent Talk

1. List three solutions given in this chapter that might be especially useful for your family.
2. Discuss: What other rewards, consequences, or fight-stoppers might be just as effective for your children?
3. Try one of these measures during the next week.

Family Time

When the family is together, initiate a reward system that you feel will be effective in curbing misbehavior. Be creative, considering each child's unique needs, problem areas, and desires (which you will appeal to with rewards).

14

A Tale of Two Myths

One more ingredient is necessary to make your home's atmosphere healthy. It is highly valued, but not easily made. We beg for it, borrow it, and always seem to need more of it. We'll craftily scheme to save it, yet we waste or lose it almost daily. Once lost, it can never be recovered. It's ironic that one of the most coveted possessions of adulthood constantly slips through our fingers like dust. That evasive, magical element? *Time.*

No one probably has less time than the busy parent of growing children, and yet I'm convinced that the care and training of those children requires more of that precious commodity than does any other job in the world.

Today, however, parents are bombarded with a stream of misinformation designed to keep one from feeling guilty if he doesn't expend much time on his parenting duties. Therefore, most parents believe one or both of two extremely popular myths. Consider these "timely" fables.

Myth Number One: "Quality" Time

A few years ago, I optimistically enrolled in one, solitary, two-hour class at a local college. The class was on a subject of great interest to me, but the workload turned out to be horrendous. I probably could have coped with it if I had not had several other "extra curricular" commitments: I was teaching childbirth classes one night a week, and Lynnette and I were making final revisions on *The Natural Childbirth Book*. In addition, some special missionary friends were in town for several weeks and needed a place to stay; their family of four (with two boys the ages of our youngsters) doubled the number of people under our roof. Then there was "family time" to consider—or there would have been, if I had not been smothered with four to five hours of homework per week for the college course. I decided to drop the course before my other responsibilities caved in.

When I presented my withdrawal slip to the instructor—a thoroughly modern woman in every way—she expressed disappointment.

"Why don't you just keep it up a while longer?" she asked. I proceeded to list the same reasons that I just enumerated above. She was unimpressed. I added that our children were only one and four, and that they needed more time with me than I was finding myself able to give.

Her reply was, "I have children, too, but they are learning that my career is a very important part of my life that they aren't going to change that fact with their demands. What about *yourself*? Don't you take any time for yourself? You know, if you do, your time with your children will be of better quality because you'll feel more fulfilled."

I told her that her course was not making me feel particularly fulfilled, only harried. (I secretly thought, *If I'm going to take real time for my self, it'll be doing my nails or making a dress—not reading this dull textbook and writing what I think of it.*) As I handed her the slip to sign, I felt sorry for her, and for her children. This lady had fallen prey to a myth that is widely circulating today, the myth of "quality" time. It tells us that the amount of *time* we spend with a child, the quantity, is not nearly as important in the long-run as the *quality* of that time.

In reality, this is like comparing apples with footballs. Time cannot be measured in anything but quantity. Time has no "quality" in and of itself. The activities that fill a segment of time can be of high quality or low, but the block of time must first exist, then be filled. If I am baking a cake that requires one cup of water, I can use many different kinds of liquids and not change the outcome much—milk, juice, sparkling spring water, or that which was first used to boil potatoes—would all produce about the same result. But if I don't put in the *full* cup of whatever liquid is used, the cake will be dry, flat, and barely edible.

I can give my children a quantity of time and make it high in quality, but I can also do neither. As one mother put it, "We must spend a large quantity of time with our children in order to capture those few moments of greatest quality."

As we've done before, let's compare this to the relationship between husband and wife. All we wives know there is no substitute for a missing husband! My husband has had occasion to spend a few nights away from home, and when I hear those creaks and bumps and thumps in the night, there is very little consolation in knowing he will be home the following morning. Even if those trips are infrequent, and even if the time he is home is of the highest quality imaginable, it does not lessen the "creepies" that come over me if I know he's not there to protect us. Quality does not make up for lack of quantity.

Creating an atmosphere of love in your home is going to take time. The ever-accelerating pace of life today has made it difficult for parents to freely take the time necessary to see that their homes (and children) are running smoothly. But when you give of your time, you are giving something no one else can offer—a part of yourself.

There must be occasions when the entire family is together, doing things as a unit, developing team spirit. There must be lots of individual attention paid to each child, to build a sense of security and value within each one. And everyone should be allowed periods to be alone in order to think, imagine, learn, and grow. Let's look more closely at these three aspects of time.

Family Time

Who can put a price tag on just "being there"? What career,

church activity, or avocation could be so important that we would let it deny us the privileges of getting to know our children intimately and becoming their friends? Of assuring them that they are important enough to spend time with? Of being their primary caregivers—the ones who train, teach, mold, set and enforce limits, kiss hurts, wield justice, and receive all the fringe benefits (kisses, hugs, and laughs)?

Many things can be rearranged to include the entire family. Setting aside one or two or four or six nights a week that you designate as "stay-home" nights will keep your family under the same roof. But you should also consider what will take place on those nights. Are there things you can do together, such as redecorating, furniture refinishing, crafts, hobbies, or homework? What can you talk about? *Plan ahead* for maximum benefits from family time.

Special Time with Each Child

These moments are almost never stumbled across in fair allotments. We have one child who is in school all day and another who doesn't even attend preschool. Jonathan gets loads of one-to-one contact with me in the course of a day, while Christopher gets less. Because Jonathan also takes a nap every afternoon, even the boys' bedtimes are the same. We try to make this up to our oldest son by making Friday nights special for him. On Fridays I will do everything in my power to prevent Jonny from taking a nap. That way he collapses right after dinner. Then we let Christopher stay up as late as Ralph and I do, joining in whatever we are doing. Often it's reading, watching TV, or playing a game. Sometimes one of us will take him to a mall or department store and leave the other parent home to enjoy the peace and quiet.

Ralph and I have found that when we have one of the boys alone, he talks to *us*, whereas, if we keep them together, they practically ignore us in favor of each other. We try frequently to split them up, to increase their contact with us. We also take great pains to keep it fair, making mental notes of who went where last and with which parent.

The more children you have, the more complex this all becomes. But it's of greater importance in a large family to make sure that each child gets time alone with both Mom and Dad. Some parents have found it helpful to keep written records of the time spent individually with each child (but do it in code or keep it out of your children's reach so they won't think your time with them is just a statistic). This will take a little additional time, of course, but it may be worthwhile, just to make sure you keep everything in perspective. You can "count" any occasion if it is a time that you and a child feel free to speak out without interference—moments in the car, outings, or dishwashing are excellent times. (I mention the latter because you can be guaranteed no one else will come within sight of the kitchen while dishes are being done.)

Private Time

Ralph Waldo Emerson said, "There was never a child so lovely but his mother was glad to get him asleep." If we translate this into "siblingese," it practically glistens with new meaning: "There was never a child so wonderful that his brother wanted to be with him all the time." Every child needs breathing space.

One day the boys had tried my patience to its limits with petty bickering and general rowdiness. Although I had no concrete proof, my "gut feeling" told me Jonathan, who was not quite three at the time, carried a little more of the responsibility for the situation. I sent him to his room (which is really "theirs") and instructed Christopher to go outside. As Jonathan got up and proceeded to march to his bedroom, a smug grin crossed his face and he said, "Good. I think I'll look at some books." It occurred to me then that his misbehavior was probably due to a case of "sibling overexposure" and he just needed some time to himself. I let him take a *stack* of books, and he stayed there over half an hour (and that's a record!).

It is very important to give each child either his own room, or at least his own private corner that is off limits to everyone else. If your children do not have the luxury of their own rooms, at least offer them exclusive use of yours during certain hours, or give each child

144

his own corner of the kitchen, den, or living room. Make it clear to the rest of the family that since there's not enough privacy to go around, any child desiring to be left alone should have his wishes respected. It's not healthy for sibling relationships to force kids to do things together.

Because of each child's need for privacy, many parents have found isolation to be the most swift, sure way to handle many sibling quarrels—"Absence makes the heart grow fonder." If the problem really is a case of sibling overexposure, this is the ideal solution. If that is not the problem, isolation at least gives everyone a chance to cool off and allows you a chance to search for possible root causes.

Myth Number Two: Independence

Dedication to all these aspects of time within a household *takes* time—time which many parents just can't seem to find. To ease the burden of guilt on parents whose lives are wrapped up in other endeavors, society has created another myth, stated something like this: "It's good for our children to be left on their own and learn to work out their own solutions to life's problems. After all, we won't always be around to take care of them." True, but this philosophy is often carried to an extreme. The proponents of this myth would have us believe that the villains of the world are those parents who remain actively involved in their children's lives and who like to control their children's environment.

How many times have you heard someone say, "We're going to put Jeremy in preschool. After all, he's almost three and he still seems so dependent"? Parents need to realize that dependency is a part of childhood. God made children this way to strengthen the family bonds at the time when the children need guidance the most. While it's true that we don't want our children to be clinging vines when they're 18, I haven't seen many that are.

Our job as parents is not to "break" our youngsters of their childhood needs and dependencies, but rather to be there as people they know they can rely on when they feel weak or vulnerable. Isn't that God's example to us?

Many children are confronted by siblings as soon as they arrive from the hospital. With such minimal experience in relationships, they cannot possibly be expected to know the right ways to handle conflicts. Just as we would never throw a child into twelve feet of water to teach him to swim, we should never take the passive, back seat approach and allow children, as one authority suggests, to "battle it out for themselves."

Likewise, when leaving children in the care of others, parents' foremost concerns should be toward the kind of care and training the children will receive in their absence. Dr. Raymond Moore writes, ". . . until the child arrives fully at the age of reason, the parent must consistently share the decision-making. This sharing should not be passed lightly to others who do not know the child and his background well and who cannot deal with him consistently on a one-to-one basis."[29]

With the financial dilemmas facing most families these days, it becomes impossible to avoid the issue of both parents working. Each family situation is different, and I have no way of knowing the details of yours, but in general it seems that mothers who work full time suffer continued feelings of guilt, inadequacy, and never having enough—you guessed it—time. It may be easy to reclaim that full-time office job six weeks after the baby is born, but many mothers have found that it just isn't necessary. I know several mothers who have used their ingenuity to develop profitable work that does not take them away from their families as a full-time job would.

If you're unhappy with your work situation, ask yourselves, as a couple, a few questions to find out why. Do we feel that our children are getting all the parental supervision and guidance they need? Are there ways we could cut corners on expenses so that our working hours could be reduced? Would it be possible for husband and wife to work different shifts, so the children could always be under the supervision of at least one parent? What about working from home—teaching a class, typing, sewing, bookkeeping, cooking for others, etc? What skills do we have that could be marketed from home?

There is usually a solution if you're willing to search hard enough. If you end up with no choice but to leave your children in the care of someone else for several hours a day, I'd like to stress again the importance of making sure that that environment is as close as possible to what you would provide for your child if you could be there. The ideal is a home-like atmosphere with a "family-sized" number of children, supervised by a mature adult whose thoughts on child-rearing parallel your own. Ask the Lord for help in finding the right person.

There is no known substitute for *time* in teaching children to love each other. It takes *time* to get to know them and understand what makes them tick. It takes *time* to set an example worthy of being followed. It takes *time* to teach and train, to arbitrate, negotiate, cooperate. It takes *time* to stop, look and listen, to label things, to keep records, to hold family conferences and devotions, and to fill charts with dozens of sticky little stars. Appropriate behavior rarely comes naturally; it is the product of a consistent example and much patient instruction. Your kids need you to be involved. Can you give the time?

Parent Talk

Evaluate together the time you spend with your children. Do you feel that it is enough? Are you satisfied with the quality of activities that fill that time? How might you grab a few extra moments with each child throughout the day? What would you do with those moments if you had them?

Recommended
Memory Verses
for Young Children

(Because of its familiarity, the King James Version has been used.)

Ephesians 5:2—Walk in love.
1 John 4:8—God is love.
Ephesians 4:32—Be ye kind.
Isaiah 43:5—Fear not, for I am with thee.
Matthew 5:14—Ye are the light of the world.
Ephesians 6:1—Children, obey your parents.
Psalm 34:14—Depart from evil, and do good.
Romans 12:21—Overcome evil with good.
Romans 12:18—Live peaceably with all men.
Romans 13:13—Let us walk honestly.
Romans 14:8—We are the Lord's.
1 Corinthians 3:9—We are laborers with God.
Galatians 6:2—Bear ye one another's burdens.
Ephesians 5:18—Be filled with the Spirit.
Ephesians 5:20—Give thanks always.
Philippians 3:1—Rejoice in the Lord.
Colossians 3:12—Put on kindness.
James 4:8—Draw nigh to God.
Proverbs 20:11—Even a child is known by his doings.
Exodus 20:12—Honour thy father and thy mother.
Psalm 34:13—Keep thy tongue from evil.

Recommended Memory Verses for Older Children and Adults

Ephesians 4:31, 32—Let all bitterness, and wrath, and anger, and clamour, and evil speaking, be put away from you, with all malice: and be ye kind one to another, tenderhearted, forgiving one another, even as God for Christ's sake hath forgiven you.

1 Thessalonians 3:12—And the Lord make you to increase and abound in love one toward another, and toward all men, even as we do toward you.

Matthew 7:12—Therefore all things whatsoever ye would that men should do to you, do ye even so to them: for this is the law and the prophets.

Romans 15:1, 2—We then that are strong ought to bear the infirmities of the weak, and not to please ourselves. Let every one of us please his neighbour for his good to edification.

Romans 14:13—Let us not therefore judge one another any more: but judge this rather, that no man put a stumbling block or an occasion to fall in his brother's way.

Philippians 4:8—Finally, brethren, whatsoever things are true, whatsoever things are honest, whatsoever things are just, whatsoever things are pure, whatsoever things are lovely, whatsoever things are of good report; if there be any virtue, and if there be any praise, think on these things.

1 Corinthians 9:19—For though I am free from all men, yet have I made myself servant unto all, that I might gain the more.

Ephesians 4:29—Let no corrupt communication proceed out of your mouth, but that which is good to the use of edifying, that it may minister grace unto the hearers.

Galatians 6:9—And let us not be weary in well doing: for in due season we shall reap, if we faint not.

Proverbs 18:19—A brother offended is harder to be won than a strong city.

Proverbs 17:22—A merry heart doeth good like a medicine: but a broken spirit drieth the bones.

Proverbs 17:9—He that covereth a transgression seeketh love; but he that repeateth a matter separateth very friends.

Matthew 12:33—Either make the tree good, and its fruit good; or else the tree corrupt, and its fruit corrupt: for the tree is known by his fruit.

Matthew 12:35, 36—A good man out of the good treasure of the heart bringeth forth good things: and an evil man out of the evil treasure bringeth forth evil things. But I say unto you, that every idle word that men shall speak, they shall give account thereof in the day of judgment.

Colossians 3:8—But now ye also put off all these; anger, wrath, malice, blasphemy, filthy communication out of your mouth.

Philippians 2:14—Do all things without murmurings and disputings.

Romans 15:5, 6—Now the God of patience and consolation grant you to be like-minded one toward another according to Christ Jesus: that ye may with one mind and one mouth glorify God.

Proverbs 15:23—A man hath joy by the answer of his mouth: and a word spoken in due season, how good is it!

Matthew 12:34—Out of the abundance of the heart the mouth speaketh.

Romans 12:18—If it be possible, as much as lieth in you, live peaceably with all men.

Romans 12:10—Be kindly affectioned one to another with brotherly love; in honour preferring one another.

1 Thessalonians 4:9—But as touching brotherly love ye need not that I write unto you: for ye yourselves are taught of God to love one another.

Galatians 5:15—But if ye bite and devour one another, take heed that ye be not consumed one of another.

1 Timothy 2:2, 3—That we may lead a quiet and peaceable life in all godliness and honesty. For this is good and acceptable in the sight of God our Saviour.

Romans 13:8—Owe no man anything, but to love one another: for he that loveth another hath fulfilled the law.

Romans 13:10—Love worketh no ill to its neighbour: therefore love is the fulfilling of the law.

Psalm 133:1—Behold, how good and how pleasant it is for brethren to dwell together in unity!

Genesis 13:8—Let there be no strife, I pray thee, between me and thee . . . for we be brethren.

Ecclesiastes 4:9, 10—Two are better than one; because they have a good reward for their labour. For if they fall, the one will lift up his fellow: but woe to him that is alone when he falleth; for he hath not another to help him up.

1 John 1:7—But if we walk in the light, as he is in the light, we have fellowship one with another, and the blood of Jesus Christ his Son cleanseth us from all sin.

2 Peter 1:5-7—Add to your faith virtue; and to virtue knowledge; and to knowledge temperance; and to temperance patience; and to

patience godliness; and to godliness brotherly kindness; and to brotherly kindness charity.

1 John 2:9—He that saith he is in the light, and hateth his brother, is in darkness even until now.

1 John 2:10—He that loveth his brother abideth in the light, and there is none occasion of stumbling in him.

James 5:16—Confess your faults one to another, and pray one for another, that ye may be healed.

James 4:11—Speak not evil one of another, brethren. He that speaketh evil of his brother, and judgeth his brother, speaketh evil of the law and judgeth the law.

Notes

[1] Niles Newton, *Family Book of Child Care* (New York: Harper and Row, 1957), p. 363.

[2] James Dobson, "A Practical Look at Love in the Home," *Focus on the Family Newsletter* (Arcadia, CA), August, 1981, p. 2.

[3] Bruce Narramore, *Why Children Misbehave* (Grand Rapids: Zondervan, 1980), pp. 11-12.

[4] James Dobson, "Coping with Sibling Rivalry" (Cassette recording), Arcadia, CA: Focus on the Family.

[5] "New Findings on Birth Order," *Seventeen* (May, 1981), p. 73.

[6] Toby Kahn, "If Your Youngest Child Is a Pain ..." *People* (August 10, 1981), pp. 90-92.

[7] Ibid.

[8] James T. Baker, "First Born Sons and Brothers' Keepers," *The Christian Century* (November 22, 1978), p. 1133.

[9] Philip Very, quoted in George E. Rowley, "How Birth Order Affects Your Personality," *The Saturday Evening Post* (November, 1980), p. 63.

[10]J. Allan Peterson, ed., *Happy Families Are Homemade* (Wheaton, IL: Family Concern, January, 1982).

[11]Robert L. Dugdale, *The Jukes* (New York: Arno Press, 1970).

[12]Paul Lee Tan, *Encyclopedia of 7700 Illustrations* (Rockville, MD: Assurance Publishers, 1979).

[13]Vivian Cadden, quoted in undated *Life* reprint, published by Childbirth Without Pain Education League, Inc., with permission from *Life*.

[14]Anne Ortlund, *Children Are Wet Cement* (Old Tappan, NJ: Fleming H. Revell, 1981), p. 54. By permission.

[15]Andrew Murray, *How to Raise Your Children for Christ* (Minneapolis: Bethany House Publishers, 1975), pp. 271-272.

[16]James Dobson, *Hide or Seek* (Old Tappan, NJ: Fleming H. Revell, 1974), p. 176.

[17]Bruce Narramore, *Help! I'm a Parent* (Grand Rapids: Zondervan, 1972), p. 164.

[18]Ibid., p. 163.

[19]Charles Swindoll, "The Scourge of Sibling Rivalry" (Cassette recording), Fullerton, CA: First Evanglical Free Church.

[20]James Dobson, "Coping with Sibling Rivalry."

[21]"Toddlers' Day Care Linked to Aggression," *The Register* (Santa Ana, CA.), August 19, 1982, p. A-10.

[22]Dorothy Singer, Jerome Singer, and Diane Zuckerman, *Teaching Television* (New York: Dial Press, 1981).

[23]Ibid.

[24]David Klein, "Ten Tips Give Parents a Guideline for TV Viewing," *The Register* (Santa Ana, CA.), July 26, 1981, p. J-1.

[25]Alan Cott, M.D., quoted in Elizabeth Scharlett, ed., *Kids Day In and Day Out* (New York: Simon and Schuster, 1979), p. 148.

154

[26]Joan Gussow, quoted in *Kids Day In and Day Out*, p. 151.

[27]Alan Cott, quoted in *Kids Day In and Day Out*, p. 149.

[28]Lendon Smith, *Feed Your Kids Right* (New York: McGraw-Hill, 1979), p. 13.

[29]Ibid., p. 165.

Other Books
You Will Want to Read